WITHDRAWN

Sins of Omission

SINS OF OMISSION

*A Primer on
Moral Indifference*

S. DENNIS FORD

FORTRESS PRESS   MINNEAPOLIS

This book is dedicated to the memory of
Helen Bourquin

SINS OF OMISSION
A Primer on Moral Indifference

Copyright © 1990 Augsburg Fortress. All rights reserved. Except for brief quotations in critical articles or reviews, no part of this book may be reproduced in any manner without prior written permission from the publisher. Write to: Permissions, Augsburg Fortress, 426 S. Fifth St., Box 1209, Minneapolis, MN 55440.

"Portrait of the Artist as a Prematurely Old Man," by Ogden Nash, from *Verses from 1929 On*, copyright © 1934 by Ogden Nash, appears by permission of Little, Brown and Company.

Cover design: Terry Bentley
Cover woodcut: Thomas or John Bewick

Library of Congress Cataloging-in-Publication Data

Ford, S. Dennis, 1947–
    Sins of omission : a primer on moral indifference / S. Dennis Ford.
        p.   cm.
    Includes bibliographical references.
    ISBN 0-8006-2401-7
    1. Christian ethics.   2. Indifferentism (Ethics)   I. Title.
BJ1251.F67   1990
241'.3—dc20   89-39163
                                                                  CIP

The paper used in this publication meets the minimum requirements of American National Standard for Information Sciences—Permanence of Paper for Printed Library Materials, ANSI Z329.48-1984.   ∞™

Manufactured in the U.S.A.   AF 1-2401
94   93   92   91   90   1   2   3   4   5   6   7   8   9   10

CONTENTS

Portrait of the Artist as a Prematurely Old Man
Ogden Nash

It is common knowledge to every schoolboy and even every Bachelor of
Arts
That all sin is divided into two parts.
One kind of sin is called a sin of commission, and that is very important,
And it is what you are doing when you are doing something you ortant,
And the other kind of sin is just the opposite and is called a sin of
omission and is equally bad in the eyes of all right-thinking people,
from Billy Sunday to Buddha.
And it consists of not having done something you shuddha.
I might as well give you my opinion of these two kinds of sin as long as,
in a way, against each other we are pitting them,
And that is, don't bother your head about sins of commission because
however sinful, they must at least be fun or else you wouldn't be
committing them.
It is the sin of omission, the second kind of sin,
That lays eggs under your skin.
The way you get really painfully bitten
Is by the insurance you haven't taken out and the checks you haven't
added up the stubs of and the appointments you haven't kept and
the bills you haven't paid and the letters you haven't written.
Also, about sins of omission there is one particularly painful lack of
beauty,
Namely, it isn't as though it had been a riotous red-letter day or night
every time you neglected to do your duty;
You didn't get a wicked forbidden thrill
Every time you let a policy lapse or forgot to pay a bill;
You didn't slap the lads in the tavern on the back and loudly cry Whee,
Let's all fail to write just one more letter before we go home, and this
round of unwritten letters is on me.
No, you never get any fun
Out of the things that you haven't done,
But there are the things I do not like to be amid,
Because the suitable things you didn't do give you a lot more trouble
than the unsuitable things you did.
The moral is that it is probably better not to sin at all, but if some kind
of sin you must be pursuing,
Well, remember to do it by doing rather than by not doing.

PREFACE

My thoughts on moral indifference grow out of both reflection on contemporary experience, shared by many, and a specific kind of reasoning, shared by a smaller circle.

Experientially, I feel an increasing sense of frustration both about moral behavior and about ethics as a practical discipline. This frustration is primarily personal, but I sense its growing presence in others as well. Feminists bemoan the recalcitrance and indifference of male chauvinists; blacks argue that America remains a racist nation despite affirmative action and equal employment opportunity; liberation ethicists persistently try to convince us that the fruits of capitalism contain a morally rotten core. This general frustration with moral indifference and the slow pace of change is reflected in the shrillness of moral rhetoric and the fragmentation of the larger moral community into factional, contentious subgroups—as if yelling from behind barricades will somehow make people listen. I don't see many people listening, and I am convinced that the conferences and workshops I attend, at church and university alike, are merely exercises in "preaching to the converted." Reflection begins in experience, and the central experience of the practicing ethicist is frustration—a frustration born in the discrepancy between an expectation of moral interest and the reality of moral indifference.

Although the experiential origin of my thoughts on moral indifference is a general sense of frustration, the intellectual origin is quite specific. "Explain the other person's mistake" has been a recurring theme throughout my education. No one deliberately makes a mistake. If we think Camus or Kant has made a mistake in his argument, we have an obligation to explain that mistake. We have an obligation to see the presumptions on which a mistaken conclusion is based. Ordinary folks, as well as philosophers, make what we view as "mistakes" not through malice, but because they see the world in a particular way. Ronald Reagan was not an evil man; from a liberal perspective, he was simply mistaken in his view of the world. Indifference may be seen as a peculiar type of mistake. So, if I rely on my education rather than my first, gut response, instead of dismissing people who are indifferent to my ideas by labeling them as capitalists or racists or mindless slugs, I have an obligation to explain their mistake from *their* perspective. Only in this way can indifference be genuinely challenged, as it were, from the inside.

The experiential and intellectual sources of *Sins of Omission* parallel the two groups for which this book is intended. First, my thoughts are addressed to anyone who shares my frustration about ethics and the moral life, to anyone who has looked around at a meeting or conference and seen only familiar faces. Whatever the particular moral issue, I hope the approach demonstrated in this book will help narrow the gap between moral expectations and the way people actually live. People are interested in all sorts of things—in baseball and rock concerts and having babies—but not many of them seem very interested in ethics. This lack of interest calls for an explanation.

Second, *Sins of Omission* is addressed to a smaller circle of persons who make the discipline of ethics their profession. For them, I present an alternative approach to doing ethics, one that begins with the absence of moral action rather than with overt expressions of evil. By beginning the work of ethics at a different point and with a different question, I hope to provide an alternative access to the discipline, one that will not only analyze but also encourage moral commitment. Because it moves beyond any specific example I might cite, a primer on moral indifference offers a methodology that is applicable to any moral issue.

I have received much good-natured kidding about the topic of this book. The standard reply to my muddled remarks about moral indifference has been, "I'm pretty much indifferent to that topic." My heartfelt thanks, then, are especially extended to four who have not been indifferent to my reflections: J. Michael West, academic editor of Fortress Press, who encouraged and guided me through the publication process; Dana Wilbanks and Davis Perkins, who read earlier versions of this manuscript; and Renee Fall, associate editor at Fortress Press, for her supervision of the book's production. In addition, I also gratefully acknowledge those listed in the bibliography whose work provided impetus to my own thoughts on moral indifference.

S. Dennis Ford
Atlanta

CHAPTER ONE

Introduction

*"The Devil's cleverest wile is to convince us
that he does not exist."—Baudelaire*

The most persistent problem about ethics is that most people could not care less. Whether the issue be nuclear arms or unemployment or care of the elderly, few people are genuinely interested; fewer still are committed enough to inconvenience themselves to work for change. The statistics alone are arresting: Every three days more people die from malnutrition and disease than from the bombing of Hiroshima. Every year more people die from preventable hunger than died in the Holocaust. Somewhere along the line, moral reflection and outrage have lost their audience. Neighbors who are otherwise decent and kind, who visit friends in hospitals and drop coins in the Salvation Army kettle at Christmastime, are, in the context of social ethics, peculiarly unmoved and indifferent. Moral hypotheses are, as William James would say, "dead," unable to make any connection between the problems of the day and our own deepest commitments. In the same way that Albert Camus once suggested that considering suicide is the beginning point of philosophy, so too considering the mystery of our own indifference is the beginning point of ethics.

Moral indifference, hardness of heart, apathy, moral sloth, a deaf ear, blindness, complacency—a variety of terms bear witness to the same phenomenon. Confronted by the nightly news with accounts of poverty and injustice, with questionable uses of technology and medical practice, how do we sustain and legitimize our continuing indifference? What enables us to move so effortlessly from the gaunt images of famine televised on the evening news to the abundance of our dinner tables? How do we anesthetize guilt? What do we permit ourselves not to see? Before ethics can address specific issues such as war and peace, economic and social justice, the environmental consequences of technology, and the rights of the unborn, it must first address this phenomenon of indifference.

The Texture of Indifference

The character of indifference changes according to its specific context. Indifference toward famine victims in Africa, for example, differs in both tone and motivation from indifference to a technological issue such as *in vitro* fertilization. Similarly, our indifference to refugees from Nicaragua or Afghanistan is not the same as our indifference to the homeless and unemployed in our own cities and towns. Indifference is a broad category whose specific meaning and source always relate to particular situations.

Despite its many forms and contexts, a preliminary definition of indifference can nevertheless be formulated: indifference is the failure either to see, to acknowledge, or to act on behalf of others.

Importantly, only the last of these categories implies an act of will, a deliberate decision, a literal unwillingness to inconvenience oneself for others. Before this point is reached, however, before one deliberately decides or fails to act, less self-conscious steps intercede. I may remain indifferent because I fail to see that a problem exists; I may not be aware that poverty lives in my own neighborhood. Similarly, I may remain indifferent because I do not see that a wide disparity between rich and poor, the haves and the have-nots, constitutes a moral as well as economic problem. Without information and knowledge about what is going on (the *is*) or without a sense that things should be different (the *ought*), I remain blind and thus ultimately indifferent to the fate of others.

In addition to seeing the *is* and the *ought* of a moral situation, I must acknowledge that the discrepancy between what is and what might be is related or somehow connected to me, to my life. I can know about exploitive labor and racial policies in South Africa, but until I acknowledge that those policies are connected to me, to my acts as an investor and consumer of South African products, I will not be compelled to change my behavior. I can pity those who are hungry, but until I recognize my participation in the creation or perpetuation of that hunger, in a life-style that is dependent on meat and such cash crops as coffee and tobacco, my moral duplicity will remain unacknowledged. Moral commitment frequently means I cannot have things both ways; I cannot enjoy the benefits of inexpensive clothes and shoes, on the one hand, while decrying the poor wages and working conditions in third-world countries on the other.

Even in those situations in which I am not personally responsible, in instances of natural disaster and past acts of discrimination, moral commitment means an acceptance of obligation. I may not be responsible for the political persecution occurring in a remote corner of the Soviet Union, but I am nevertheless obligated to do whatever I can to end it. I may not be responsible for deciding whether someone should be removed from a life-support system, but I am nevertheless obligated to be concerned. By accepting that obligation, I acknowledge my membership in a single, ongoing, human community. In addition to *seeing*, then, ethics requires an *acknowledgment* that I am connected to others in a way that entails obligation, regardless of my personal responsibility.

The unself-conscious "decision" to remain indifferent, not to see or acknowledge a moral obligation, is not individual in nature. Indifference cannot be blamed, and thus dismissed, on inherently "bad" people. Admittedly, in specific instances, individuals may remain indifferent because of personal cowardice, lack of experience, or physical or spiritual exhaustion. Essentially, however, indifference is a social, transpersonal phenomenon. Persons do not individually decide to remain indifferent; they are indifferent because they have— as participants in their culture and local communities—inherited ideas, rituals, mythologies, stories, and methods that foster or legitimize indifference rather than commitment. We acquire indifference in the same way that we acquire language: unself-consciously, without deliberation or malice, almost innocently.

It is to these cultural and transpersonal components of indifference that succeeding chapters will most frequently turn. How do we become aware of a moral issue and imperative? Given the same situation, why do some people see a moral issue while others do not? What is the meaning of citizenship as participation in a moral community? What stories have we adopted to express our deepest convictions about ourselves and our obligations toward others? Do these stories encourage or impede an acknowledgment of moral involvement? How is our conception of God and the church related to our propensity either to remain indifferent or to come to the aid of others?

The answers to such questions directly support or undermine indifference. Indifference is all of a piece and multifaceted; it represents the convergence of a number of disparate cultural factors. As a result, it cannot be explored apart from a correspondingly interdisciplinary study of popular culture, theology, and the history of ideas. In succeeding chapters, therefore, I will look briefly at a variety of disciplines in tracing the roots of moral indifference. Exposing the roots of indifference through description and analysis is a necessary first step to its eventual diminution.

Discerning What Is Not There.   Traditionally ethics, as reflection on moral behavior, emphasizes the sins of *commission* rather than the sins of *omission*. It usually concerns overtly "wrong" actions, rather than inaction or indifference. Thus, as is seen in our legal system, persons can be prosecuted for drowning someone but not for letting someone drown. Physicians are currently embroiled in controversies that turn precisely on this point: Overt murder is clearly unacceptable, but under what circumstances are they permitted to let someone die? Killing an innocent child would elicit moral condemnation, but our culpability in permitting thousands of children to die from preventable disease is unclear. Ethical theories that concentrate on deliberate, overt action have difficulty in helping us with those situations when the failure to act is morally culpable.

Importantly, an emphasis on moral action, and the sins of commission, implies a morally innocent universe in which nothing is "wrong" until some morally reprehensible act is committed. In the Eden narrative, for example, paradise is violated by a deliberate act of disobedience. Until Adam and Eve ate the apple, the question of sin, much less of indifference, was unintelligible. In an innocent, static world, not acting—doing no harm—can be a virtue.

Unfortunately, we no longer live in paradise. Deplorable conditions exist and persist because of our indifference. Ethics must acknowledge this less-than-perfect, more dramatic context, in which—as the phrase of the 1960s expressed it—"if you are not part of the solution, you are part of the problem." By doing nothing, Adam and Eve might have remained blameless, but in our world doing nothing is itself morally reprehensible.

Doing nothing in situations that demand action, precisely the sins of omission, is the heretofore invisible side of ethical reflection. Methodologically, indifference reveals that evil frequently occurs not because of deliberate wrong decisions, but because the process of deliberate decision making may be preempted altogether. The central question is not why people decide wrongly but why a situation does not present itself as a moral issue or imperative. The question, "Why do people act immorally?" is replaced by the obverse question, "Why do people fail to act morally?" This is to approach ethics by a *via negativa,* comparable to the astronomer's study of black holes. Black holes, like indifference, can be detected only by observing what is not there, by seeing nothing where there should be something. Apart from such a propaedeutic study, indifference threatens to become the black hole of ethics, engulfing every moral issue into a lightless, motionless state of complacency.

A Confession of Having Left Things Undone.   Ethical thought is insistently contextual. Apart from particular contexts, the universal dos and don'ts—the "thou shalt nots"—are empty and without application. In liberation theology, to cite the most obvious example, emphasis on political freedom and economic justice cannot be understood apart from the conditions of deprivation, powerlessness, and oppression from which it emerges. Any approach to liberation ethics, and by extension, any ethic apart from its indigenous context, is inherently flawed.

I am a white, heterosexual male Protestant who enjoys a level of economic and educational privilege beyond the imagination of most of the world's inhabitants. Because of this privileged position, I am disqualified from speaking authentically about liberation or, for that matter, about feminist or gay ethics. The situation of the poor person or the homosexual or the feminist is not my situation, and to pretend otherwise constitutes an evasion and denial of my own moral situation and responsibility. Presumedly, every situation is indigenously moral, including my own. I should not have to leave my situation, either actually or imaginatively, to practice ethics. Indeed, any ethics that requires me to become a voyageur—whether a revolutionary, a business executive, an illegal alien, or some other— should, for that reason alone, be suspect.

My situation is one of relative comfort and security. I can pretend no other. Day in, day out, my horizon of experience is reasonably comfortable and secure. Given this situation, the moralist is led to ask: What moral issue is most central, most indigenous to comfort, relative financial security, and ease? What issue most clearly expresses the moral problem confronting those placed within that situation? Stated in this way, the answer to the question is surely indifference. For members of the middle class, moral issues such as the threat of nuclear war, environmental pollution, reverse discrimination, and, for some, school prayer and abortion, are certainly indigenous and genuine. But the central issue, the most persistent, fundamental, and recalcitrant issue, is indifference itself.

The ultimate situation of the middle class is that it can afford not to become involved; it is free to remain indifferent. If my local environment becomes polluted with hazardous chemicals or crime, I can move away. If the local school does not teach my children what I wish, I can put my children into private schools. If I am threatened by the specter of nuclear war, I can protest, write letters, and watch the Redskins on television. Doing nothing carries no immediate penalty; I can remain indifferent with complete impunity. Indeed, if I do become involved, if I become so involved that I begin to sacrifice my otherwise comfortable life, my peers will call me a radical, a fanatic, a nut. Indifference speaks to and expresses the complacent condition of the middle class as does no other issue. It is the issue through which all others must first pass.

Adopting the words of Romans 7:16, the Book of Common Prayer contains the liturgical confession of the indifferent: "We confess that we have sinned against thee . . . by what we have left undone. We have not loved thee with our whole heart; we have not loved our neighbors as ourselves." A country-western lyric expresses the same sentiment in a more popular genre. In the song, a man bemoans the loss of his sweetheart. He reflects that he didn't do any of the things that country-western songs have made famous. He didn't cheat, he didn't drink or gamble, he didn't squander his paycheck in honkie-tonk saloons. He lost his sweetheart, not because of what he did but because of what he didn't do. He didn't tell her he loved her. He didn't hold her at night. He didn't kiss her good-bye in the morning. As he laments, "It's not what I did, it's what I didn't do."

Whether expressed in liturgy or a country-western song, indifference is the moral failure of those who confess that "It's not what I did, it's what I didn't do." It's not that I cheat on my wife or my taxes. I don't steal from my neighbor. I don't engage in unethical business practices, and I don't advocate nuclear war. No, my failure is not attributable to what I do; it's attributable to the black hole of what I don't do. In small and large ways alike, I am unwilling to inconvenience myself for others.

In a dramatic, fallen world, inaction as well as action demands reflection and explanation. The confession of having left things undone is quickly followed by a question: Why? Why are people not interested in and committed to moral issues? Why does evil continue to flourish among good and well-meaning people? Why do ethical decisions fail to attract a sustained interest by students and the public at large? Why do moral issues gain recognition and then fade in popularity like the latest song? Who, in these times, will inconvenience themselves significantly in order to help others?

The Enchantments of Indifference

Indifference occurs whenever we fail to *see* or *acknowledge*, and thus fail to *act* on, a moral imperative. A failure to see or acknowledge is attributable, at least in part, to the myths of indifference through which we see and interpret experience. I use the term *myth* broadly here, to refer not only to traditional sacred stories but also to narratives, presumptions, concepts, ideologies, and popular entertainments as well. Myth is a functional term; anything that serves as a model for the orientation of understanding, behavior, or attitude is by definition mythical. Myths are classically associated with stories of gods and goddesses. At one time in our cultural past these stories provided a means for interpreting experience. In our own day, however, the mythical function is more often than not performed by popular stories or ideologies.

Take, for example, the popular myth that "people get what they deserve." As we will see shortly, the myth of fairness or justice is reinforced by countless stories of people ascending from rags to riches through virtue, hard work, and perseverance. We want the world to be fair, and the myth of fairness perfectly fulfills our deepest desires. Aesop told the story of the ant and the grasshopper to illustrate that those who work prosper and survive the winter, while those who do not, perish. The fate of both the grasshopper and the ant is directly and justly tied to what each did or did not do. The ant prospered because he worked and prepared for the winter; the grasshopper perished because he played. The myth tutors us in the presumption that each receives what he or she fairly deserves.

The myth of just rewards, when used as a model for interpreting social experience, is an exemplary myth of indifference. On the level of seeing, the myth of just rewards simply tells us "how things are." It tells us that some people are poorer than others and that the distinction between rich and poor is merited and fair. Through the auspices of the myth, we presume the world is fair and that large discrepancies between rich and poor are natural in the same way that the sky is blue. As a consequence, we seldom question or see the contribution of luck, malice, genetics, and social structures either to the failure of others or to our own success. Schooled on the old fable of the ant and grasshopper and its many successors, the myth of fairness and justice encourages and legitimizes social indifference. We see the is-ness of poverty, perhaps, but we fail to see the discrepancy between things as they are and things as they might or ought to be.

Myths function most powerfully when they are accepted un-wittingly. The most powerful myths are also the most invisible. In such instances, myths bewitch us into equating perception with reality. As through a camera's eye, we see with the myth, while the myth itself remains unnoticed and taken for granted. We seldom self-consciously decide to remain indifferent to the needy. More likely, we simply fail to acknowledge responsibility or respond because we perceive that the needy "deserve" their poverty because, we presume, they are lazy, unintelligent, or sexually promiscuous. The world is just and poverty is justly merited. On the one hand, the myth provides a self-conscious rationale or excuse whenever a moral obligation be-comes inconvenient. It completes the sentence, "I don't want to help the needy because. . . ." On the other hand, the myth—by persuading us that poverty is merited—disconnects us from acknowledging moral responsibility. Indifference is not attributable to a general malaise or the failure of a religious ethic after the death of God. On the contrary, indifference is attributable to a tenacious, largely unself-conscious commitment to the "myths of indifference" in whose enchantments we live and interpret experience.

Myths tend to lose their power over perception whenever the presumptions and images they convey become explicit and self-con-scious. The enchantment of myth dims whenever it is recognized that the myth expresses not reality itself but one of many possible interpretations of experience. The myth that people get what they deserve is called into question if it can be demonstrated that much poverty is unearned by hapless children and industrious persons working full time for a minimum, substandard wage. Through the process of analysis—historical, sociological, and philosophical—myths are debunked in such a way as to weaken their influence. Through analysis, largely unconscious presumptions about how the world is gradually become conscious and explicit, a matter of choice rather than a matter of unwitting inheritance.

Indifference thus is linked to our commitment to "myths of indifference." If this is so, then the analysis and consequent debunking of such myths will serve to free us from their enchantments. Pre-sumedly many well-meaning persons are indifferent not because they have self-consciously and deliberately said to themselves, "Those people are needy and I don't care." More often, I think, people are indifferent because they are committed to the myth that people get what they deserve. Otherwise well-meaning people can be freed from the enchantment of indifference if the presumptions, ideologies, and images conveyed by the myths of indifference can be made explicit and visible. Once seen, persons may self-consciously choose to be indifferent but more often, we hope, well-meaning people, when confronted with unwitting indifference, will choose to be committed.

Myths and Absences

An analysis of three representative myths of indifference constitutes the subject of chapters 3, 4, and 5. Understanding myths is essential to seeing the *is* and *ought* of moral situations, as well as to acknowledging the connections between those situations and my own life. As such, they rightly occupy a major portion of this study.

In chapter 3, I analyze the myths of indifference associated with religion. Common opinion links religion with moral commitment but, ironically, religion (and its theological underpinnings) frequently legitimizes indifference to social ethics. The silence of the gathered assemblies on moral issues is often deafening. How, in particular, popularized expressions of evangelical and liberal forms of Christianity succeeded in fostering indifference is the subject of my initial comments.

Chapters 4 and 5 extend the style of analysis begun in chapter 3 from religion to the realms of popular culture and the history of ideas. In chapter 4, I examine several of the myths current in popular culture, specifically the stories of success, the American cowboy, and the story of having no story. Popular culture both expresses and tutors us in what we most often take for granted. What we take for granted, our "common sense" if you will, defines the status quo of a recalcitrant indifference. We give shape and meaning to our actions and inaction with the myths of popular culture; that being the case, the question informing chapter 4 is, "Which stories of our cultural heritage contribute to moral indifference and how?"

Chapter 5 continues the work of chapter 4 by examining the political and philosophical roots of indifference. Like popular culture, a nation's political philosophy or ideology expresses what social arrangements are taken for granted. Our obligation to help others, our presumptions about what is and is not important, are encapsulated in the formal and informal documents of a public philosophy. The public philosophy of contemporary America frequently contributes to indifference and moral sloth, and in chapter 5, I demonstrate how and why this is so by tracing the political notion of freedom. Again, the intention of chapter 5, as of chapters 3 and 4, is deliberately debunking. By making explicit the presumptions, stories, and ideologies of popular religion, culture, and public philosophy, I hope to lessen their enchantments.

I said earlier that indifference is, at least in part, attributable to myths of indifference. In chapters 2, 6, and 7, I address those parts that fall outside the immediate realm of myth. In addressing these areas, I both continue the task of analysis and move forward to a more constructive ethic. In the end, the problem of how indifference can be overcome includes a positive as well as a negative movement.

In chapter 2, I provide a historical and psychological context for the problem of indifference. Even if indifference can be attributed to various myths of indifference, the question remains why we un- wittingly "choose" these myths rather than the myths of commitment. Before it is expressed as moral indifference, sloth is a fundamental human tendency. A review of how the ethicist Reinhold Niebuhr and his successors have understood this tendency provides a clue to the *willingness* of our enchantment.

Chapters 5 and 6 take a more constructive approach to resolving the problem of indifference. It is crucial that, through analysis, the enchantment of indifference be broken. But, having accomplished that task, the problem of indifference remains. The constructive task requires asking the question: "What happens when moral commit- ment succeeds and why?" By answering this question, we define those elements that, if absent, contribute to moral indifference and, if present, provide a framework for making specific suggestions about how moral commitment may be nurtured and strengthened.

In chapter 6, then, I develop a more theoretical account of moral commitment in which I propose that moral commitment represents the integration of experience (both actual and imaginative), moral frameworks of interpretation, and power/embodiment. These three categories expand the more preliminary categories of seeing, ac- knowledging, and acting that I introduced earlier. As I will develop in chapter 6, experience provides a basis for seeing, just as moral frameworks of interpretation provide a basis for acknowledging or owning moral obligation. Finally, the notion of power/embodiment— as both an independent element and the *telos,* or goal, of experience and moral frameworks of interpretation—completes our theoretical account of what needs to be present before moral commitment is fulfilled. The absence of any one of these three elements contributes to moral indifference.

In chapter 7, I extend and apply the conceptual framework developed in chapter 6 to three levels, or arenas, of moral engage- ment—the personal, the political, and the intermediate. As we shall see, each of these levels has its characteristic absences and sources of moral indifference. A theoretical account of moral indifference proves its usefulness by helping us identify absences in the moral demands of day-to-day living.

Chapter 8 summarizes the course of our argument by looking at indifference from a rhetorical perspective. The word *ethics* in the chapter title is deliberately ambiguous. The failure of ethics in America is, in the first instance, a failure of moral behavior. In the second instance, however, it is also a failure of ethicists to engage an audience in moral concerns and issues. I close by suggesting that the identification of what is lacking in instances of moral indifference provides a clue to a more effective rhetorical strategy for ethicists.

The aims of this brief work are both practical and necessarily modest. As a preliminary work, it seeks to be provocative and neither intends nor claims to be exhaustive. The myths and ideas of indifference that I examine are merely representative or illustrative of an approach to the problem of moral indifference. I do not attempt to identify or describe all the myths of indifference (as if I could) or, for that matter, to trace the history of those myths. The study is *necessarily* modest because the acceptance of inconvenience on behalf of others is finally a mystery. No foolproof technique exists for making persons more committed to social ethics, just as no technique exists for making persons fall in love. The approach and suggestions expressed here are continually humbled by the real-life examples of those many people who work in soup kitchens, build homes for the poor, organize for social change, and otherwise help others unselfishly.

Words are no substitute for actions; nevertheless, I hope my reflections directly participate in the tasks of social ethics. At least in intention, this work is insistently practical; by understanding the problem of indifference, I hope to call attention to an often overlooked impediment to social commitment. The benefit of this book will lie in a new perspective and especially in the moral actions of those who are persuaded by its perspective.

For the middle class, ethics begins with reflection on inaction, on what we do not do. A consideration of indifference precedes an examination of more specific issues such as racism or nuclear arms, just as background precedes foreground. This study prepares the way and thus participates in more direct forms of action. It begins ethics at a new point, indifference; it calls attention to and offers an explanation for moral indifference; it undermines several of its enchantments, and it offers suggestions for how one goes about identifying those elements that, if absent, contribute to moral indifference. Without the *telos* (goal) of *praxis* (action) constantly in mind, writing— and reading—this book is itself an avoidance rather than a propaedeutic, and thus merely another expression of moral indifference.

CHAPTER TWO

Sloth:
The Basis of Indifference

Sloth, that archaic and ugly-sounding word, denotes a universal tendency toward inaction that, on occasion, takes the form of moral indifference. Not all sloth is moral indifference, but all moral indifference expresses and is an aspect of sloth. A preliminary discussion of sloth thus provides a historical antecedent and context for succeeding chapters on moral indifference.

Sloth plays a prominent, if often unspoken, role in ethics, regardless of the specific issue. Most people are not heroically or self-consciously greedy, lustful, or envious. A handful of people conduct the arms race; a smaller handful are active players in a complex issue such as in vitro fertilization. Nevertheless, greed, lust, and envy flourish because most of us do not care, because most of us are simply unwilling to inconvenience ourselves for change. However archaic it may sound, sloth is very much a contemporary problem.

Both the seriousness and persistence of sloth were acknowledged by sloth's early inclusion as one of the seven deadly sins. The tradition of the deadly sins, as well as common experience, attests to sloth's universality. Despite its enduring presence, however, sloth has largely been ignored by contemporary ethicists. Who among prominent twentieth-century ethicists, for example, has explicitly dealt with the problem? The only possible answer to that question is Reinhold Niebuhr. Almost singularly, Niebuhr articulated the experience and effects of sloth for his generation. Especially in his discussions of the sin of sensuality, Niebuhr described the nature of sloth in both its individual and collective manifestations. Thus the work of Niebuhr and, as we will see, his more popular successors provides a rudimentary introduction to our subject. In subsequent chapters we will focus on how sloth is specifically expressed as moral indifference; in this chapter, however, our focus is on sloth as a fundamental human tendency, before it is shaped by particular contexts and ideologies into the specific form of sloth known as moral indifference.

Reinhold Niebuhr and the
Sin of Sensuality

Anxiety: The Precondition of Sin.   Niebuhr's anthropology is most clearly expressed in his two-volume classic, *The Nature and Destiny of Man*. According to Niebuhr, humanity stands at the juncture of two realms, the natural and the spiritual. On the one hand, the human being is a naked ape who is limited by, and often subject to, the vicissitudes of nature. Each person is born, lives, and dies like other animals and, like them, is driven by impulse, subrational fear, and aggression. When compared to the needs of hunger and sex, the protection of offspring, and the pain of injury, the trappings of civilization are fragile and ephemeral. At base, that is, most essentially, we are passive creatures, not enlightened and in control of our own destiny but driven first this way, then that, by dark forces beyond our control. We think we are in control of history, but not so. The arms race, for example, goes on unabated, despite its irrationality. We think our lives are orderly and sane, and then we learn that our best friend has run off with her secretary to Bermuda.

While being biological creatures, we are also spiritual creatures created in the image of God. If we are animals, we are not merely animals but spiritual beings capable of using, as Niebuhr says, the "forces and processes of nature creatively." In defiance of all forms of reductionism, humans use their reason, memory, and hope to extricate themselves from the causal necessities of nature and the subconscious to create that "new level of reality which we know as human history." Humankind is passive and acted upon, to be sure, but also acts independently and autonomously to offset and transform the environment. No other animal has mastered fire, or written a book, or created art, or rocketed to the moon; no other animal has created laws to protect the weak, or devised the means for world destruction. As creatures, humans are subject to nature and finitude but, as spiritual beings, they are capable of freedom, transcendence, and liberation from the given.

According to Niebuhr, history, for both the individual and Western civilization, is a story of increasing freedom. Just as a child moves from dependency to autonomy, so too humanity has moved from the undifferentiated harmonies of nature to a complex freedom, symbolically from the simplicity of nature to the pluralism and choice of the city. The Reformation, Renaissance, and the rise of what Niebuhr termed "bourgeois civilization" combined to create and nurture an emergent sense of individual freedom and responsibility. The Reformation's doctrine of the priesthood of all believers contributed to the belief that individuals were accountable to God alone and thus were capable of transcending the norms and dictates of their particular nation or church. Similarly, the Renaissance and the later success of experimental science emphasized the preeminence of reason over revelation and tradition. Equipped with the tool of reason, humans no longer had to accept passively the truths of religious or monarchical authority. And finally, the creation of bourgeois culture and a mercantile class encouraged and rewarded individual initiative and resourcefulness. More and more, the givenness and accidents of birth and place were replaced by the history one made for oneself, with the result that the future became more important than the past, experience more important than dogma.

Niebuhr's history narrates a story of increasing freedom and initiative, a congruence between the emergence of consciousness and genuine moral action. The triumphant note of that history, however, is quickly followed by a corresponding fall, a deliberate evasion or "escape from freedom" at the very moment of its achievement. As in all great tragedies, the source of humanity's greatness is also the source of its eventual destruction, for the same freedom that establishes the possibility of genuine history and moral action also creates confusion and anxiety. The central problem revealed by history lies in the duality of human nature, in Niebuhr's words, in human "finiteness and freedom." Neither creatures entirely of nature nor entirely of spirit, human beings are estranged from themselves and can accept themselves fully neither as animals nor as children of God.

Experientially, the human position between finiteness and freedom creates anxiety. Anxiety, Niebuhr states succinctly, is the "inevitable concomitant of the paradox of finiteness and freedom." Anxiety is both humanity's privileged state and its burden, but, in any case, it is a state that humans can never accept. By attempting to escape anxiety, humans attempt to become that which they are not, and thus sin. Anxiety is the precondition of sin, for the basis of temptation lies in the inclination to deny either the contingencies, limitations, and impulses of finiteness or the reason, responsibility, and freedom humanity possesses as a genuine spirit created in the image of God.

The anxiety that is the human condition can be alleviated by denying either our finiteness or our freedom. If, on the one hand, we deny our finiteness and limits—if, for example, we assume that our thoughts are godlike in both their universality and virtue—then we fall victim to the sin of pride. If, on the other hand, we deny our freedom, if we passively accept the status quo or submerge ourselves in the vitalities and necessities of nature, then we fall victim to sloth or what Niebuhr termed the sin of sensuality. Although Niebuhr is justifiably famous for his analysis of pride, his often neglected discussion of its counterpart, sensuality, provides insight into the equally prominent sin of sloth.

The Sins of Sensuality.   For Niebuhr, sensuality is the escape and submergence of the anxious self into the realms of finitude. It is important to repeat that unadorned definition at the outset because the term *sensuality* easily deceives the unwary who identify it exclusively with sexuality, lust, and the love of physical pleasure. A distinction must be made between the manner or means through which anxiety is escaped and the act or non-act of escaping. If the sin of sensuality is limited to physical impulse and desire, then its relevance to a willing submission to ideologies, persons, and institutions, to its social as well as individual manifestations, is obscured.

Niebuhr's discussion of sensuality includes a number of specific examples—sexual license, gluttony, extravagance, drunkenness, and lust, among others. Niebuhr concludes that sensuality has two primary forms—the sensuality of idolatry and the sensuality of nothingness. Both forms of sensuality describe and thematize the experience of sloth, and—although both forms of sensuality begin with the individual—both have far-reaching social consequences.

The Sin of Idolatry.   Niebuhr argued that the sensuality of idolatry occurs whenever the anxious self denies its freedom through the deification of and subjugation of itself to some "other," whether that other be an ideology, a person, a political movement, or an institution. The victim of idolatry escapes his or her anxiety by accepting the wishes and dictates of someone or something that is conceived to be more powerful, wiser, or more real than oneself. In this way, the doubt, anxiety, and necessary skepticism of critical thought are replaced by the simplicity and assurance of a childlike primitivism.

Although the roots of this sin are found in the experience of individuals, the sin can nevertheless have dramatic social consequences. In his own day, Niebuhr found the sin best exemplified by Nazi Germany and its veneration of the Führer and the motherland. Mass movements, then as now, are seductive because of their ability to reduce the anxiety that we experience as limited yet thinking creatures.

More recently, the sin of idolatry has become an analytical tool in feminist thought. It is, for example, proper and appropriate for women to help meet the demands of raising a family and supporting a spouse. But if that support leads to a denial of women's legitimate desires and aspirations, if women can only see themselves in relation to men, if—instead of thinking for herself and being an equal partner in marriage—a woman passively defers all decisions to her husband and sacrifices her desires in order to fulfill his, then the virtue of self-giving becomes distorted. In such instances the virtue of giving becomes a means for avoiding responsibility and women become or remain victims of what scholar Susan Nelson Dunfee has appropriately labeled the "sin of hiding."

Idolatrous forms of sensuality reflect a willingness to forget the extent to which we have created the world in which we live. Humanity creates technologies and culture, political systems and ideologies, but then becomes so alienated from its own creations that they usurp human sovereignty. Unable to accept the anxiety that is the concomitant of responsibility and freedom, we willingly accept the notions that "You cannot beat the system," "You can't stop progress," and "Business has to make a profit." The arms race, surely, is the clearest example of a false consciousness. The arms we have created have become our masters, to which we dedicate larger and larger portions of our time and resources. Supported by the ideology of national security and the communist threat, we passively acquiesce to expert opinion and what "must be done." To acknowledge that each of us is partially responsible for the arms race, that the threat of nuclear annihilation is at least partially our doing, is overwhelming. As a consequence, it is much easier and comforting to ignore the issues altogether by attributing to the systems we have created an unassailable recalcitrance. That is "just the way it is," we say, and to think otherwise is unrealistic and utopian. Victims of false consciousness are slothful heirs to a persistent tendency in human nature.

A similar method for ignoring our responsibility involves attributing human problems to the recalcitrance of nature. For example, the problem of hunger is attributed to natural disasters and bad luck rather than to the unequal distribution of resources and the appropriation of arable land for cash crops. Similarly, if underdevelopment can be attributed to racially inherent traits of laziness or lower intelligence, if we cannot do anything against the natural impulses of sex and aggression, then we are excused from efforts to amend what is beyond our control. We tell ourselves that it is only human nature to be aggressive, that societies operate to ensure the survival of the fittest, that altruism is not natural—with such phrases, an ideology of what is "natural" legitimizes competition, indifference to "losers," and an economic system of rewards and punishments even for such basic necessities as food and shelter. Surely nature does constitute a limit to our human endeavors, as Niebuhr (among others) reminds us. But just as surely nature is invoked apologetically in a way that legitimizes our slothful indifference.

The Sensuality of Nothingness.   The submergence of the self to the other—whether that "other" be an ideology, a person, or nature— is frequently succeeded by a disabling disillusionment. According to Niebuhr, whenever this occurs, idealism is replaced by cynicism and the self takes flight "not to a false God but to Nothingness." On the individual level, the flight to nothingness is acted out in a willing submission to pure sensuality, that great and overwhelming power in which the self is annihilated and reduced to a mere "grain in the tremendous heave that lifted the grass blade its little height." The passion to forget, to overwhelm anxiety and the still small voice of conscience, to live perfectly free of inhibitions and taboos, undisturbed by thought in a hedonistic paradise, creates a tremendous market for drugs, entertainment, and the sexual exploitation of both sexes. "The lost weekend" has entered our common parlance for good reason; it accurately describes and articulates the deepest desires of the sensuality of nothingness.

On a social level, Niebuhr argued that the flight to nothingness is an expression of philosophical despair over either the world's manifest imperfections or the futility of ever arriving at "the truth" amid a host of fragmentary, partial viewpoints. If truth and goodness are relative, why pursue them? If all acts are morally equal, why do anything that is inconvenient? If attempts to figure things out, to get at the truth of what is good and right, are confusing, why not abandon serious thought about such issues altogether? It is much simpler not to think at all about such inherently contestable, unanswerable questions, or mindlessly to adopt someone else's answers. Nihilism or, alternatively, a hopeless idealism, is a constant threat. Niebuhr describes complete skepticism as an "abyss of meaninglessness." Within that abyss, commitments are either uncertain and unfounded or fanatical and unyielding, but in neither case do they express that delicate balance between finiteness and freedom indigenous to being human.

Beyond the flight to nothingness represented by pure sensuality and moral nihilism, the sensuality of nothingness is also expressed as a recalcitrant complacency. Complacency is indifference squared, a self-satisfied, unassailable, even arrogant form of indifference. Complacency is an inert self-satisfaction. Niebuhr found an example of such complacency in the actions of the liberals of his day. Faced with the threat of Nazism immediately preceding World War II, liberalism was incapable of imagining the evil actions and intentions of the Third Reich. Insulated by their own preconceptions from a realistic appraisal of the situation, the Western nations were incapable of believing that Hitler would actually invade the Scandinavian countries or, in quick succession, France. How could such a preposterous, absurd little man constitute a threat? What Niebuhr terms the "complacency of the obligatory" occurs whenever a group becomes comfortable and secure to the point of losing contact with actuality. The powerful can afford to stay comfortably submerged in the routines of life precisely because they can do so with impunity. Without daily reminders of a wide discrepancy between expectation and reality, the powerful lack an inherent context for moral reflection and are thus vulnerable to the complacent sloth of nothingness.

The emergence of consciousness and the emergence of genuine morality are, for Niebuhr, congruent. Genuine morality requires the maintenance of a delicate balance between finitude and freedom and a concomitant acceptance of anxiety as an inescapable condition of being human. Sloth occurs whenever we escape our anxiety and responsibility by willingly submerging our consciousness into the finitudes of sensuality, mindless idolatries, or the comfortable routines and complacency of daily life.

Sloth in Public Discussion

Niebuhr's description of the sin of sensuality provided an occasion for renewing a consideration of sloth and its expression as moral indifference. Oddly enough, however, such a consideration was not adopted by his professional or academic colleagues. Instead, the subject of sloth was more often taken up by authors addressing a wider or more popular audience. Typically, these authors considered sloth from the perspectives of sociology, physiology, and psychology—as well as theology. By adopting these various perspectives, Niebuhr's

successors perceived and described additional dimensions to the phenomenon of sloth.

The Problem of Indifference.   The study of indifference is predicated on the belief that indifference constitutes a genuine problem.
Problems in ethics, as in other realms, arise when a discrepancy occurs
between facts and value-driven expectations. Indifference occurs as
a problem whenever we expect persons to care and to act on behalf
of others, and they do not. If an elderly person stumbles in the street,
we expect passersby to stop and help. If a local steel plant closes, we
expect the community to support the unemployed. Without the value
and expectation of caring, inaction in itself would not be problematic.
We do, however, expect persons to care, and the discrepancy between
that expectation and inaction transforms indifference into a genuine
problem.

The problem of indifference can be solved in one of two ways.
On the one hand, if persons act on behalf of others, if they are indeed
willing to inconvenience themselves on behalf of others, then reality
conforms to our highest ideals. The expectation of commitment is
fulfilled, and indifference does not occur as a problem. Alternatively,
indifference will fail to materialize if we abandon our expectations
that people should care. If what is simply is, if all values are derived
from culture and all culture is mere invention, then normative statements, *oughts,* are expressions of will and power rather than of discovery and obedience. If we not only do not but cannot legitimately
expect persons to care because the world is finally meaningless, then
inaction in the face of need is no problem. Positivism and nihilism,
or the experience of utter hopelessness, undermine value-driven expectations and thus reduce the possibility that a discrepancy will occur
between facts and values. Without expectations, lethargy is not a
problem; what "is" overwhelms what might or "ought" to be. The
term *indifference* may still be applicable descriptively, but evaluatively
it has lost its meaning.

The Sin of Sloth.   *Indifference* not only identifies a problem; it
identifies a tendency, as well. Persons do not make the decision to
be or not to be indifferent from neutral ground; on the contrary, they
are inclined not to care. The house odds are always in favor of
indifference; there is always more than a fifty-fifty chance that lethargy
will overcome committed action. Whatever the issue, whether it be
nuclear arms or the evils of communism or the morality of premarital
sex, there is a tendency to say—with our actions, if not with our

words—"Who cares?" Historically, this deep-seated tendency toward indifference is associated with the cardinal sin of sloth.

In its symptoms, sloth has physical and spiritual aspects. Originally referring to the neglect of religious duties within the monastery, the term gradually broadened in application. Physically, sloth is associated with laziness, sleep, idleness, indolence, lethargy, inattention, and death. In continuity with these physical characteristics, sloth as a spiritual malady is associated with complacency, boredom, affectlessness, apathy, ennui, paralysis of the will, gradual withdrawal from society, holding back, and lack of joy in response to God's creation. The stasis of sloth is not a happy or peaceful state; tellingly, sloth is also associated with an abiding sense of melancholy and a restlessness of spirit. Etymologically, *sloth* is a translation of the medieval Latin term *acedia,* meaning "without care."

The Dynamics of Sloth. Various metaphors have been used to describe and interpret sloth: psychological, physiological, theological, and social. Psychologically, sloth is described as a sin of arrested childhood; sloth extends into adulthood the passivity, dependency, and egocentricity characteristic of childhood. Children are disenfranchised citizens of the adult world. As such, they have little control over their environment. Children do not choose what they eat or where they live or what clothes they wear. Their world is given, not created, and children have little choice but to accept what their parents, as gods of old, bestow. Children must wait on other people to do for them. Given this disenfranchised status, the passivity of childhood is entirely appropriate. When extended into adulthood, however, such passivity provides a context for indifference, a slothful expectation that someone else will do it for us.

In contrast to children, adults inhabit the world that they help to create. Children must accept the inevitability, the givenness, of war or hunger; adults, however, accept nothing as inevitable or beyond their control. The history of civilization, like the history of individuals, is the story of how the given has been transformed into the created. Thus the premodern givens of disease, of monarchy, of religious taboos, and of slavery have given way in the modern era to health care, democracy, the Enlightenment, and emancipation. In the process, what was at first regarded as given and inevitable became a human artifact and thus a human responsibility. Twenty years ago, infertility was a given, beyond the realm of medical science to correct. With *in vitro* fertilization, however, fertility yields more and more to scientific technique. If the world is a human artifact and if, especially in the social realm, what we find is what we have created, then to refuse to participate in the act of world-creation, to accept passively the status quo, or to expect others to effect necessary change represents a refusal to accept the responsibilities of adulthood as well. Inextricably, we must—because we already do—participate in world-creation. Rejection of that imperative in favor of the passivity of childhood indicates arrested development and sloth.

In addition to passivity, sloth frequently displays a childlike egocentricity in which its victims can only see and act on behalf of their own self-interest. If passivity is the characteristic response of sloth, egocentrism and narcissism represent its characteristic goals. Victims of sloth may not be merely passive; indeed, they may be very active in initiating change or even incidentally improving conditions for others. However, if such activity is driven by egocentricity, if its purpose is merely self-aggrandizement, then its perpetrators are nevertheless victims of sloth.

Adulthood is an expanding circle of responsibility. To be an adult means to accept responsibility not only for oneself but for others as well, including future generations. Egocentric people are not without care, but they are slothful because the circle of their care is too small, too egocentric. Sloth is associated with the neglect of duty and, ultimately, with withdrawal from others. Egocentric persons exhibit both qualities; they neglect duty toward others and, by their self-centeredness, they separate themselves from the community in a way that leads to melancholy. Thus those who are egocentric, no less than those who are passive, embody the slothful sins of extended childhood.

Physiologically, sloth is sometimes characterized as a defective form of love. In comparison to the other sins, indifference lacks all passion and affection. It is a life deprived of *eros*. Greed, lust, gluttony, envy—these are sins because in them the passion for things is placed above the desire for God. Sloth is the most terrifying and recalcitrant of sins because it is defined not by misplaced passion but by a lack of desire altogether. It is thus, as William May describes it, "the shadow of death," a passionless state for those living without expectation or *eros* in a colorless world after the death of God.

According to a popular saying, the opposite of love is not hate but indifference. Which is more difficult, to change someone's opinion or to make someone care? Does sloth precede caring, is it the state from which we start? Or is it the spent remains of caring for the wrong objects, a condition of exhaustion for those who have cared too much and too often for that which is other than God? The completely slothful person is immune to other sins, but he or she is also immune from *eros* of the good. Sloth is, as Dorothy Sayers describes it, the sin that "believes in nothing, cares for nothing, seeks to know nothing, interferes with nothing, enjoys nothing, hates nothing, finds purpose in nothing, lives for nothing, and remains alive because there is nothing for which it will die." As such, it is the sin of a defective, inoperative love.

Sloth, again physiologically, is sometimes interpreted as a form of physical revulsion. Confronted by scenes of a nuclear holocaust, whether in our imaginations or as presented in such widely heralded television movies as *The Day After* and *Testament,* the human soul seems literally incapable of taking in so much horror and destruction. Whenever we try to think about nuclear war, we are arrested and feel sick, whereas when we deny our predicament we feel well again and can go about our normal routines. This sense of well-being, based as it is on denial, is a form of insanity because it represents the failure to act in the face of an overwhelming danger. It is, according to Jonathan Schell, as though "everyone had been sedated." The path to world destruction, he goes on to say, is one of progressive "enervation, dulled senses, enfeebled will, stupor, and final paralysis." The nausea of sloth is especially active in a nuclear age. The habit of denial that originates with the nuclear issue becomes a way of life; unable to face the "most important reality of our time," we are equally unable to face the more mundane realities of daily life. If we can successfully deny the nuclear issue, we can successfully deny the needs of our next-door neighbor as well.

From a theological perspective, sloth is the sin that most directly bears witness to the need for salvation and to the difficulty of grasping the meaning of salvation existentially. With lust, it is often difficult to perceive what it is that one needs to be delivered from. Lust, like most sin, is intrinsically attractive and seductive. Sloth is unique because it is inherently unattractive; indeed, it has been described as the only sin for which payment is not deferred. No one seeks or decides to become indifferent, to live in a passionless, restless state of noncaring. Sloth is not chosen; on the contrary, it seems to choose and hold its victims captive. To be saved from lust feels like a form of deprivation (or a lack of opportunity); to be delivered from sloth, however, attests to the spirit-filled, enlivening nature of redemption. Deliverance from sloth represents a convergence of moral conversion and religious salvation. We are, moralistically, saved from sin but we are also saved from the restless apathy and boredom of the slothful.

Thus, within a traditional context, the sin of sloth is a summons to a fuller life. The coin of sloth, flipped over, yields the possibility that life can be active rather than passive, caring rather than self-centered, energetic rather than listless.

The seriousness of sin is predicated on the esteem and potential of the soul. We are meant to care that forty thousand children die each day from preventable diseases, and when we do not, we have somehow missed the mark. To fall victim to sloth is not only an act of disobedience, a lack of response to God's good creation, but an act of betrayal toward one's true and final potential. Achievement of one's potential is an extraordinary achievement precisely because human nature, after the fall, contains the tendency to be indifferent. Moral commitment is an unnatural state and yet, as tradition attests, such unnaturalness is required to achieve our true and best natures.

The Social Context of Sloth.   Characterizations of sloth—whether psychological, physiological, or theological—frequently neglect the social context within which sloth is nurtured. Even though sloth is an inherent tendency, social arrangements can either encourage or discourage the extent to which that tendency is realized.

In *The Seven Deadly Sins: Society and Evil,* Stanford Lyman recalls the familiar ways in which modern urban life, work, and leisure contribute to an attitude of noncaring. Lyman reminds us that social mobility—the abandonment of family and community for the sake of education and career advancement—fosters a "community" of strangers. In contrast to more traditional communities, the deliberate communities of modernity are established on the fragile basis of accident, common interests, and utility. Commitment to one's neighbor is less if that neighbor is temporary, belongs to a different church, and pursues different interests and occupations in locations far removed from one's own. The isolation of urban life, the insulation of neighbor from neighbor, and the undermining of common purposes by the plurality indigenous to the city contribute to the feeling of indifference. If the neighbors do not belong to the same groups as I, if they are not from the same part of the country, did not attend the same schools, and have no friends in common with me, then why should I care? What do their lives have to do with mine? If, as Aristotle observed, the good citizen is inseparable from the good community, then the breakdown of traditional communities also represents a breakdown of the morally committed individual.

The alienation characteristic of the urban setting is characteristic of the modern workplace as well. The bureaucratic character of large corporations, the fragmentation of work into increasingly narrow sub-specialties, and the reduction of all value to the single dimension of profit serve to alienate workers from the products of his or her own labor. Commitment to what I do is reduced if I cannot see the effects of my labors, if my senses are dulled by routine and standardization, or if the job at which I labor in no way expresses who I am as a person. We get through the day, but our commitments and rewards are frequently only financial in nature.

Schooled daily in the ineffectiveness and meagerness of our contributions and frustrated by the lack of response we find in bureaucracies (whether corporate or political), we become disheartened in the work of citizenship as well. If the experience of modern work teaches us that work is dull, unfulfilling, and a matter of technique rather than meaning, why should our commitment to public policy be any different? What is the point of working on public policy when what I do does not matter, politicians do not listen, and political systems are unresponsive to change? The work of affecting public policy, like all work, seems unrewarding and futile. In this context, it comes as little surprise that the number of persons voting in our presidential elections has steadily declined during this century.

Third, and lastly, modernity has robbed leisure of its recreative power. Too frequently, the plethora of things available to an affluent middle class dulls the senses and satiates all interest and desire. Boredom, too, is an aspect of sloth. Vacations and days off are experienced as interminable, empty, or wasted by an addiction to frantic sports or mindless pursuits. Encouraged and seduced by the entertainment industry, we waste and become lost in our free time rather than use it to transform and improve our communities. We are sedated into inertia. We never have time, and yet time is always on our hands. Because we are alienated from our work, leisure is seen as merely an opportunity to escape occupation, rather than an opportunity to express freely and to create who we are. The community languishes, while we watch the latest episode of *Dallas*.

Moral sloth is a persistent and deep-seated tendency. The fulfillment of that tendency, however, is especially likely whenever the community is fragmented, work seems alien, or leisure is reduced to entertainment.

Remedying Sloth

The power by which sloth and moral indifference hold us is demonstrated by their very invisibility. As Baudelaire once said, "The Devil's cleverest wile is to convince us that he does not exist." Possibly no other area that touches on so many aspects of our common life has been so neglected. A cursory review of Niebuhr and his successors introduces themes that will recur in various forms throughout the course of this study.

Most importantly, Niebuhr's discussion of the human condition refocuses attention on sloth as a beginning point of moral reflection and action. Sloth, along with its moral expression as indifference, is not an eccentric or temporary interest; on the contrary, it is a fundamental human tendency against which every moral issue must battle. Idolatry and the "lost weekend" or, in Niebuhr's terms, the "sins of idolatry and the sin of nothingness" are not aberrations but constant temptations. Sloth has been described in a variety of ways—one of the seven deadly sins, a case of arrested development, an example of defective love, and an instance of physical revulsion, among others. Each of these descriptions identifies absence of action—sloth and its expression as indifference—as a central and persistent problem of the moral life.

Occasionally, descriptions of sloth suggest remedies. If indifference represents a social pathology in the way suggested by Lyman, then it can be reduced by strengthening communities and by lessening the degree of political and occupational alienation. More often than not, however, indifference is described in ways that fail to indicate practical solutions. If indifference and sloth are rooted in human anxiety or defective love, how does one practically go about solving the problem? Anxiety, as used by Niebuhr, describes a human condition rather than a problem readily amenable to solution.

The insights of Niebuhr and others recall our attention to a central and neglected area of the moral life. But their descriptions of sloth and indifference lack obvious prescriptions. Frustrated by a lack of practical remedies, my own reflection on indifference takes a different, perhaps less philosophical turn by attributing indifference to what I described earlier as "myths of indifference." We will now turn to the analysis and debunking of representative myths from religion, popular culture, and public life as a practical first step in overcoming moral indifference.

CHAPTER THREE

Religion:
The Theology of Indifference

Indifference has many sources: political, psychological, and social. Tragically, however, one of its most persistent sources is theological and religious. Legitimized by what at times seems like divine counsel, theologically informed indifference is especially venomous and resistant to change. I may be indifferent, but if that indifference is sanctified by God, then who can challenge me?

The question of religiously inspired indifference has been most explicitly addressed by members of the evangelical community. In examining what Timothy L. Smith has characterized as the "Great Reversal," evangelicals have repeatedly wondered why and how their community moved from a position at the forefront of social reform to a position of social paralysis. Most of us contemplate a moral issue from an initial standpoint of relative neutrality. We may or may not decide to become committed. In contrast, evangelicals began with a moral imperative, informed by a rich historical and theological heritage epitomized by the Social Gospel movement in the late nineteenth century. Given such a promising beginning, what in the evangelical heritage contributed to the eventual emergence of moral indifference? The answer to that question provides an introduction both to a theology of indifference and to themes that recur in different guises throughout this study.

A recent generation of evangelicals, including Jim Wallis, Paul Henry, and David O. Moberg, has identified a number of impediments to an evangelical commitment to social ethics. Below, I summarize the discussions of this generation under the four areas of *the optional church, Bible, dualism,* and *individualism.* Each of these four areas contributes to the mythology of indifference indigenous to evangelicals. Liberals, however, should not find comfort in this discussion. Theological liberals also exhibit their own form of indifference, one—I might add—that is less frequently confessed. In a concluding section, therefore, I will briefly examine the impediments to liberal social involvement, realizing that at times we are heirs to both forms of theological indifference.

The Optional Church

The first impediment to evangelical social commitment involves a particular conception of the church. Historically, views about the church were influenced by and in turn influenced the American political revolution. Not surprisingly, therefore, the purpose and nature of ecclesiastical and political communities have often been seen analogously.

The question, Is there salvation outside the church? finds its political counterpart in the question, Is it necessary to be a citizen of the republic? Is the church community, like the community at large, a hindrance to personal growth, a heap of useless and confining conventions, or is it a necessary context for growth and maturity? Is the church a voluntary association that one can choose to join or not? Or is it, as a more conventional notion would have it, a divine community that is prior to the individual, outside of which there is no salvation?

In Protestant America, that is, in the America that celebrates the individualism of Thoreau, Emerson, and Whitman, the answer to those questions is clear. Institutions, whether they be political or ecclesiastical, are secondary to the needs, autonomy, and self-determination of the individual. Individuals are essentially presocial or asocial; they exist prior to and independent of the community until such time as they choose to enter into a social contract. At best, institutions are necessary evils that demand adherence to societal norms in exchange for mutual protection and prosperity. At worst, institutions create a totally alienated environment in which societal roles and expectations replace all sense of self. Apart from institutions, individuals are essentially good and innocent; once involved in institutions, however, individuals share in a steady encrustation of corrupting influences.

Theologically, the Reformation proclaimed that God can be encountered face to face, individually, without intervention or mediation of the community or institutional church. Salvation through faith rather than works meant that spontaneous and essentially private experiences of the holy were more authoritative signs of grace than adherence to the institutional, objective norms prescribed in creeds and dogmas. In the tradition of my youth, all that is necessary for salvation is summarized in John 3:16. The church is not needed to mediate communication with God or to define the tasks through which salvation can be assured. Once a sacred and irreplaceable institution, the church became a possibly helpful but in no sense essential institution. Participation in the church was considered voluntary and optional; there was salvation outside the church in a way that made the church ultimately superfluous.

Institutionally, the optional church is best expressed by the revival meeting. The evangelical tradition is identified with tent meetings and revivals conducted by itinerant evangelists or circuit riders with neither institutional nor denominational loyalties. Today, this tradition's best-known and most vocal proponents are cast in the mold of Billy Graham, Oral Roberts, and television evangelists such as Pat Robertson. Evangelicals conduct a "meeting," rather than a gathering of the congregation. The defining mission of such revival meetings is not the gathering of the faithful or the administration of sacraments but the conversion of individuals. Success of the revival is not measured by institutional change, such as the extent to which the church has affected public policy, but by how many individuals are confronted by the Word in such a way that a decision for or against Christ becomes inescapable.

Methodologically, the central act of bringing persons to this confrontation is the preaching of the Word. Importantly, therefore, neither the objective of the revival meeting (the conversion of individuals) nor the means (the preaching of the Word) calls for institutional change, affiliation, or embodiment. Conversion and change of any kind do not, according to this model, depend on institutions; they depend on a change of heart in the individual. Thus the effects and possibilities of institutional change and structures are obscured.

The preacher, who is called to proclaim the Word, is likewise only marginally related to the institutional church. The "preacher" replaces the traditional offices and functions of the "priest." The preacher is most often seen as a prophet who, not unlike the members of his or her congregation, is not subject to the restraints and compromises of institutional roles. The authority of the preacher does not reside in an ordained, institutionalized office, nor is it necessarily due to long years of theological training. On the contrary, the authority of the preacher rests on his or her ability to preach the Word effectively. Ultimately, however, even this authority is undermined by the belief that if one is guided by the Holy Spirit then guidance from even the preacher is superfluous. Indeed, reliance on the clergy means to approach one's faith second-handedly; it denies the individual's direct experience with God. According to the revival, the priesthood of all believers is thoroughly democratic; ultimately the preacher or minister has no more authority than the layperson. Stripped of his or her sacramental status and office, the minister's authority rests entirely on the option of the congregation.

Traditionally the church was regarded as a sacred institution, a divine community established by God, apart from which salvation was not possible. Membership in this community was not voluntary in a way that affirmed the priority of the church and its ministers over the wishes and desires of the individual. With the Reformation and the American Revolution, however, conceptions of the church, its nature and mission, changed. The ability to confront God directly, without mediation; the belief in the priority, even nobility of individuals outside the corrupting influences of institutions; the evangelicals' emphasis on the revival and on itinerant preachers apart from institutional affiliation and embodiment—each of these factors conspired to create a context for the optional church. No longer a sacred, indispensable institution, neither the church nor its servants could maintain a compelling moral authority. As a result, the church's challenge to indifference was undermined.

Moral action is inconvenient. To avoid that inconvenience, we need a framework that justifies our indifference. The necessity of acknowledging the moral demands of the church wanes to the extent that we see the church as optional. If, for example, the church accuses me of conspicuous consumption while others go hungry, I can proclaim—with theologically sound reasons—that neither the church nor its servants has the authority to judge. I can choose for or against living within the church's dictates without violating my individual relationship to God. Ultimately I do not need the church to assure my salvation. Consequently, if either the church or its ministers begin to make me uncomfortable, if its imperatives become inconvenient, I can change to a less unsettling minister or join a less demanding church or abandon the institutional church altogether. Secure in the knowledge that individuals are prior to institutions, I can judge the church in a way that renders my membership optional. The optional church lacks a compelling moral authority, and I can always choose to leave. Consequently, I can dismiss any of the church's imperatives at the point at which they become inconvenient. The individual stands invulnerable, alone before God. Alone, that is, except for the Bible.

The Bible

For evangelicals, the authority of the Bible is inversely related to the authority of the church. As church authority receded, the authority of the Bible became preeminent. Luther confronted the church of his day on the basis of *sola scriptura,* scripture alone. Evangelicals are, with good reason, identified as the people of the Book.

Evangelical use of and reliance on the Bible is detrimental to social commitment in at least three ways. First, given the context of the optional church as just described, the authority of the Bible resides in the authority of its interpreter, whether that interpretation be simple common sense or subtle, informed historical research. Even if the supposed lack of interpretative consensus on what the Bible means is not as great as skeptics would claim, a background noise of interpretative differences nevertheless serves to undermine the compelling authority of scripture whenever it becomes uncomfortably demanding. Adoption of any single interpretation of scripture is, like the church itself, optional. Scripture, as well as the church, exists within a pluralistic context. Passages about feeding the hungry can be undermined by saying that they represent a minor aspect of Christ's ministry or, by a sleight of hand, that they refer to spiritual nourishment rather than the physical sustenance we each require. Analogous to a direct, unmediated experience of God or the holy, the Protestant principle assures me that my contact with God's Word is likewise unmediated. Guided by the Holy Spirit, I am irrefutable.

Even without a plurality of interpretations, evangelical reliance on the Bible contributes—secondly—to social inactivity by not addressing contemporary moral issues directly. The foreign policy of the United States, the morality of nuclear arms and nuclear power plants, the theological implications of genetic engineering and computers—these issues were not part of the context in which the Bible was written. Persons who rely on the Bible for explicit moral guidance can therefore dismiss such issues as not being an aspect of their religious commitments, as literally being nonbiblical. Not surprisingly, therefore, people of the Book are likely to concentrate on the enduring, personal sins of greed and lust rather than on such context-specific issues as genetic engineering or disposal of nuclear wastes. The Bible's failure to address a moral issue, to deal explicitly with such issues as the morality of alternative technologies and economic systems, contributes subtly to their being ignored altogether. Informed by the Bible alone, evangelicals can comfortably ignore and dismiss the disturbing issues of the day.

Alternatively, the absence of clear biblical warrants for specific moral actions may lead the devout to abandon the search for moral clarity altogether. At best, biblically based moral guidance can be achieved only by the dubious and fallible method of extrapolation and abstraction from one context to another context far removed in time and circumstance from its original setting. If we are accustomed to clear directions, introduction of an issue not contained in the Bible can result in a sense of confusion and loss of direction fatal to our search for moral guidance. Confronted with an uncomfortable demand, I can say, with perfect humility, that no one can be certain of his or her interpretation, that everyone must decide for himself or herself alone.

Historically, evangelical theology has favored apocalyptic parts of the Bible. Reliance on such passages constitutes a third way in which the Bible has contributed to moral indifference. According to popular interpretation, apocalyptic sections foretell a time of tribulation before the triumphant return of Christ. Ironically, "bad" times are in fact good precisely because they herald the near arrival of the new age. In the context of the imminent arrival of the kingdom, efforts for social reform are deemed useless or in conflict with God's plan. Bad times are either a sign of the imminent end of time or an expression of God's will. In neither case is the course of history amenable to moral action, however well intentioned. History and social situations are not within the control of humans but of God alone. Given this context, the options are either to wait patiently or, better still, to convert others to Christ in the brief time remaining.

A plurality of interpretations, the restricted pertinence of the ancient texts when understood literally, and the selection of apocalyptic passages—these are but three ways in which the evangelicals' use of the Bible contributes to indifference. Confronted with an issue such as the social effects of computers, I can—within this context—dismiss accusations of indifference by claiming that this issue is nonbiblical, is subject to unclear and conflicting interpretations or applications of scripture, and finally is not important in light of the imminent end of the age. Fortified by such sanctions, my comfortable indifference is unchallenged.

Dualism

Dualism supposes the universality of opposites as a framework of explanation. Good and evil, light and dark, reason and emotion, subject and object, freedom and determinism—such dualisms persist as rudimentary categories from which thought can begin. Dualistic tendencies run throughout Christian history, in ancient Manichean and Gnostic thought, in the doctrines of Augustine and Luther concerning the two kingdoms, in the voluntary separation of a saving remnant from the corrupting seductions of the world. To be sure, such dualisms have been challenged by more orthodox, monistic doctrines that suppose a unity of source, or nature, beneath apparent dualities. Such challenges, however, have failed to persuade evangelicals for, in the main, they have remained staunchly dualistic. One such dualism has contributed particularly to evangelical indifference: the dualism of body and spirit.

The dualism of material and spiritual, of body and soul, is commonplace and archetypal. According to this dualistic framework, two distinct realms of being exist. On the one hand is the physical, tangible realm of material bodies that is subject to extension, time, and decay. On the other hand is the transcendent, eternal realm of the spirit that is pure, timeless, and ontologically preeminent. In the material realm, persons suffer, grow old, and die; in the spiritual realm, they live forever in a pure and incorruptible state. Persons are indisputably *in* the material world and thus subject to its contingencies, but they are properly not *of* this world. Within their material bodies there dwells an eternal soul. It is this soul that is essential and of ultimate importance; all the rest is chaff.

Because persons are properly concerned with ultimate spiritual things, the proper collective concerns of the church are spiritual as well. The task of the church is accordingly not the ordinary, human task of feeding the hungry and caring for the sick; on the contrary, it is the very special and uniquely spiritual task of saving souls, of bringing persons from the realm of the material into the realm of the spiritual. The church has a moral imperative to fulfill the task that only it can perform. Other institutions and governmental agencies can care for the material needs of the poor and dispirited; only the church, however, can attend to the souls of women and men.

As a "spiritual" community with a uniquely specialized mission, the church and its members are "above" the turmoil and divisiveness of earthly "politics." Debates about exploitive labor practices, the material conditions of the poor, the tax code, the threat of nuclear annihilation are secondary, "political" problems because they deal with material concerns, which are not, by definition, the concerns of the church. Rich and poor, free and enslaved, communist and social democrat, dove and hawk—all are in need of personal salvation. Christ came not as a revolutionary but as a redeemer. As long as the church is unimpeded in propagating its saving message, it can work within and encompass any social, political, or economic context or position. With few exceptions, therefore, any position is acceptable or at least tolerated. The church wants to be inclusive; it does not wish to exclude anyone. As a result, commitment to potentially divisive social issues always represents an intrusion and diversion from the universal and spiritual church.

In the realm of economics, the dualism between body and spirit has legitimized indifference to the poor by defining economic and financial matters as exclusively material in nature. Because these matters are material in nature, and thus ultimately unimportant, persons can accumulate material possessions without a sense of guilt or social obligation to those less fortunate. Wide discrepancies between the rich and the poor can be ignored because "the important things—that is, the spiritual things—in life are free." If persons are not to be thought less of because they are poor, then neither are they to be thought less of because they are rich. Unfettered from their economic entanglements by the dualism between the material and the spiritual, the rich are permitted the unrestrained pursuit of (spiritual) virtue without (material, social) ethics. Dualism sustains indifference by reassuring us that there is no contradiction between being both a conspicuous consumer and a Christian.

Informed by a perspective that separates the material from the spiritual, inconvenient demands can be readily dismissed. If I am asked to make a commitment on behalf of disarmament, I can excuse my lethargy by categorizing the issue as "political" and thus secondary in importance. It is not the church's concern, and it is potentially divisive. If, alternatively, I am made uneasy by the effects of racism, I can comfort myself with the belief that human beings are finally inviolable, beyond the reach of how they are treated in this world. Certain people may be poor in body or even persecuted, but they rest safe in the arms of the Lord. If I am uneasy with wealth, if I am bothered that persons in my community are either rich or poor, then I can reassure myself that material inequity really is unimportant. This (material) world will soon pass away. As night gives way to day, so this world will give way to the spiritual world to come.

Historically, the central dualism between body and soul that serves so readily to legitimize indifference found expression in the equally dualistic division that occurred between liberals and evangelicals. To the extent that social concerns became identified with liberalism, it became practically impossible to remain both socially concerned and theologically evangelical. Although dualism is a philosophical question, its historical expression in the split that occurred between liberalism and evangelicalism represents a second reason it has contributed to the social indifference of evangelicals.

Theological liberalism emerged and gained prominence during the late nineteenth century as a response and accommodation to the increasing preeminence and success of the empirical sciences. Like those sciences, liberal theology was uncomfortable with the supernatural realm of divine Being and intervention. Insistently inductive, liberal theology rejected the authority of tradition and sacred texts in favor of the direct authority of experience. Above all, liberalism stressed the continuity between the human and the divine—the immanence, not the transcendence of the divine in human affairs.

Liberalism's emphasis on the horizontal, material dimension of religion encouraged the development of social ethics. Unable to rely on supernatural intervention and optimistic about humanity's ability to perform good, liberal theologians urged people to rely on their own natural resources. According to liberalism, it is humanity's responsibility and duty to create a better world. If God acts, it is indirectly, through the actions of men and women. Because God is immanent, or hidden, liberal theologians accepted the Christian ethic and social program without accepting the accompanying commitment to traditional ontology or doctrine. Inductively, the Christian is not easily distinguished from the non-Christian; the religious person is not easily distinguished from the reform-minded socialist; the priest is not easily distinguished from the concerned social worker. Good will—regardless of its motivating source—replaces the good news as a central theological doctrine.

For evangelicals, liberalism's accommodation to science and the secular age represents an abandonment of the supernatural core of religion. In essence, liberalism is a failure of ontological nerve. Religion is nothing if it is not about a supernatural, eternally changeless God who can and must intervene in history because of humanity's fundamental incapacity, after the fall, to do good. Within an evangelical context, liberal pronouncements on the Social Gospel are seen both as naively optimistic, a denial of the fall, and as a means of avoiding the central scandal of the Christian message. What is more, because it emphasizes the corporal rather than the spiritual condition of humanity, liberalism succeeds in confusing the secondary with that which is of primary importance.

For evangelicals, the theological and doctrinal challenges of liberalism became paramount. In the face of those challenges, evangelicals could no longer unself-consciously assume their faith. On the contrary, evangelicals increasingly felt obligated to defend their faith against the incursions of modernity. Energy and attention necessarily shifted from an initial involvement with the Social Gospel to theological combat. In combating liberalism's immanent doctrines, evangelicals placed greater and greater emphasis on God's transcendence, sin's corruption, and humanity's inability to save itself through social reform. Given what became the either-or choice between promoting the Social Gospel or the "real" gospel, between saving bodies and saving souls, between commitment to this world and commitment to the next, evangelicals chose the latter and thus increasingly separated themselves from the social imperatives that had earlier characterized their tradition. Certainly, it is not impossible to be both evangelical and committed to social ethics, as more recent events have shown. Historically, however, the close identification between social movements and theological liberalism defined the context for the Great Reversal. As an ascendant liberalism pushed evangelicals from the center to the periphery of social and theological influence, evangelicals retreated from their former positions at the forefront of social reform.

Dualism is a persistent problem within the church. The dualism implied in separatist movements and the compartmentalization of life into church and business, the sacred and the profane, are additional examples that come readily to mind. Central to any such discussion, however, is the dualism between the spiritual and the material and its historical expression in the conflict between liberals and evangelicals. Informed by a dualistic perspective, I can, if called upon to inconvenience myself on behalf of others, dismiss the challenge by saying that the issue is ultimately unimportant, not a function of the spiritual church, or not conducive to a unified Christian community. Dualism thus serves to legitimate my continuing indifference.

Individualism

Individualism is the most subtle impediment to social ethics because it informs a studied, unself-conscious blindness to social problems and obligations. Because of individualism, the question of my obligation to political refugees from Central America, not to mention my obligation to those closer to home, never arises or becomes an issue about which I have to make a decision. Because of individualism, indifference is not the result of a deliberate decision, but a corollary of how I see the world.

Individualism locates the source of all value and worth within the individual. With the possible exception of the nuclear family, one's primary obligations and duties pertain to satisfying one's own needs and desires. In comparison to the natural and preeminent status of the individual, social institutions are artificial, secondary, functional arrangements between aggregates of individuals. The legitimacy of these social arrangements rests on their ability to satisfy individual desires. The individual, as a result, has no inherent or indissoluble obligation to the group. Participation in the group is voluntary, a social contract that remains in effect only so long as the group serves the needs of the individual.

Individualism places a premium on autonomy, self-reliance, and freedom from the inconvenience and constraining effects of societal obligations. As a social philosophy, individualism finds expression in a deep-seated reluctance to carpool and to share lawnmowers. Somehow the "right" of others to infringe on my freedom is less than my right to pursue my own individual interests and self-fulfillment. I can choose to help others, but I am not obligated to do so. Inconvenient obligations of whatever kind can be dismissed by remembering that no one has a right to violate my privacy and right of self-determination. Freedom, in this context, means the absence of any kind of restraint.

Individualism serves to define the parameters within which justice and fairness are ordained. Everyone is responsible for himself or herself alone. If a person fails, it is that person's responsibility alone; it is not the responsibility or fault of the economic or social system. According to the philosophy of individualism, everyone starts at the same place and advances on the basis of merit. Even within the family, the economic disparity between brothers can be great without embarrassment or contradiction because individualism attributes responsibility and success to the individual. If my brother is greatly more successful or greatly less successful than I am, it is not my concern. Because of individualism, our fates are unrelated. I am not responsible for him, nor he for me.

Placed within a theological context, the central affirmation of an individualized faith is that religion is ultimately a private matter. A religion informed by individualism emphasizes saving individual souls rather than ushering in the kingdom of God; in short, it is a private, rather than a corporate or political, religion. As we have seen earlier, within the Protestant tradition, human beings confront God face to face individually, without the intervention of church, state, or priest. Accordingly, only God can judge my actions and the status of my salvation. Positively, the Protestant principle is liberating in that I do not have to accept the judgments of others. Negatively, however, its freedom contains the seeds of license and irresponsibility.

Because I cannot be judged by others, I am free to do whatever I wish. No social obligation or censure can ultimately impose itself between me and my God.

Partially at least, the evangelicals' inability to see the institutional dimension of social problems is attributable to their definition of and response to sin. Informed by the perspective of individualism, evangelicals trace social problems to the sins of individuals. Thus, problems of unemployment, economic inequality, abortion, and teenage pregnancies can be attributed to the individual sins of greed, sloth, and lust. The solution to the drug problem rests with the individual "just saying no." The individual thief is at fault, rather than the conditions that make theft inevitable. Social problems can be ignored because they stem from the sins of individuals. Change the individual and society will change; without a change of heart in individuals, larger social change is impossible. We cannot, as has often been said, legislate morality. What seems like evangelical indifference to social ethics is, from the perspective of individualism, merely illusory. Evangelicals are concerned with social ethics. Their seeming indifference merely reflects a decidedly individualistic approach to social problems, one that sees both the source and solution to social problems in the conversion of individual hearts.

Individualism, understood as the autonomy of one person from the next, is legitimized by a presumption that God rewards the good and righteous and punishes the wicked and sinful on an individual basis. Persons are poor because they are lazy; children have children because they are sexually immoral. Evangelicals are not totally blind to inequalities; however, such inequalities are legitimized because God guarantees justice for the individual, if not in this world then in the next. A theological presumption of God's unerring justice toward individuals is more detrimental than and predates Social Darwinism. Social Darwinists understand themselves as the fittest, without necessarily assuming to be the most virtuous. Proponents of the doctrine that God rewards the virtuous, however, assume their success is attributable to their own righteousness. Consequently, they cannot only take pleasure in their success, they can also take comfort and satisfaction in the knowledge that they are the most righteous of persons. Those less advantaged, on the other hand, are doubly cursed: they lack both worldly success and godly favor.

From one perspective, individualism is an eminently pragmatic theological doctrine. I cannot affect systematic change directly; I can only change myself. Individuals, as individuals, cannot stop the pollution of the environment or nuclear war; individuals can, however, control their own behavior. The proposition that one is responsible for factors over which one is not in direct control has always met with limited acceptance. What is more, the individual behavior in question is normally unambiguous in a way that one's participation in social sins is not. Thus, a person is clearly drunk or unfaithful to a degree that his or her involvement and culpability in economic or racial exploitation are not. I am in control of and responsible for my personal actions in a way that is not as true, or at least not as clear, as when I am participating in a group.

Informed by individualism, tutored by the conviction that everyone is responsible for himself or herself alone, convinced that the world is just, and assured that sin is ultimately rooted in individualized forms of vice, we—as a people—are unschooled and unpracticed in the arts and vocabulary of politics and social ethics. The effects that groups and institutions have on individuals and the possibilities that exist for group action and reform become less clear within the context of individualism. The ultimate triumph of individualism is expressed by the inability not only to see the social dimension of sin but by the inability even to raise the issue of social obligation. I see the world via individualism and, because I see the world that way, I fail to acknowledge my obligation to others.

The Impediments of Liberalism

A survey of the theological impediments to social ethics would be incomplete without a further glance at liberalism. As we have mentioned, liberalism is often associated with a variety of social movements and thus would seem an unlikely candidate for impeding social ethics. Liberalism's emphasis on divine immanence, coupled with its faith in scientific progress and the ability of humans to reason together for mutual benefit, stands in sharp contrast to the more pessimistic, transcendent view of the evangelicals. Nevertheless, liberalism can and does contribute to social indifference in at least three ways.

First, liberalism frequently provides warrants for denying individual responsibility. Rightly, liberals discern the systematic nature of ethical problems and the limitation of individual actions toward solving global problems. My eating less meat will not solve the problem of hunger in Africa; providing food baskets at Christmas will not alleviate poverty in the inner city; demonstrating at my local post office will not reduce the likelihood of nuclear war. Social (legislative or political) action is the means of remedying social problems; in contrast, individual action, one person helping another person directly, is easily dismissed as being merely a temporary "Band-Aid" solution.

Liberalism's emphasis on social action and institutional change is a necessary corrective to an evangelical emphasis on individuals. However, such an emphasis can too quickly become an apologetic for indifference. Uncomfortable with an obligation to help another in response to a direct and immediate appeal, the "Band-Aid" label permits me to dismiss my obligation. It can excuse my failure to contribute to famine relief and to the Red Cross because, after all, such temporary aid does not really get at the problem. Similarly, my concern for global issues in South Africa can permit me comfortably to ignore more local, inconvenient situations closer to home. While saving the world, I may neglect to save the neighbor next door. If dualism contributes to virtue without ethics, liberalism can result in ethics without virtue.

Second, social action on the part of Christians, whether liberal or evangelical, can appear to those outside the church as amateurish and not very effective. The various peace movements, for example, have not been notably successful. In the context of the experts, Christians who study the defense establishment seem naive or idealistic, and consequently are not accepted as seriously informed participants in the public debate. In the face of such criticism, liberals, as well as evangelicals, may retreat into their own compounds. Too easily, the failure to be effective spokespersons, to translate beliefs into public policy effectively, is dismissed with the phrase that "our mission is not to be successful but to be faithful." Certainly that phrase contains a grain of truth, but when used too readily it can excuse a form of cultural solipsism and self-righteousness that encourages an indifference to *effective* social action.

Third, and finally, the liberal church suffers from a lack of ontological, transcendent imperatives and warrants for its actions. Because of their skeptical Enlightenment attitude toward biblical authority and the church, liberals have little to compel them to do things that they do not otherwise want to do. Transcendence offers a radical critique of the status quo that is not otherwise available. Without the possibility of a qualitatively different revelation, of transcendent aid and assurance in otherwise hopeless situations, liberalism has difficulty in consistently maintaining the hope that defies mere realism. Deprived of a transcendent faith, what would the civil rights movement or the struggle for liberation have accomplished? Third-world and liberation theologies are characteristically evangelical in orientation precisely because ontological warrants are an essential ingredient in their struggles. Apart from such warrants, expediency and convenience—if frequently perceived as realism—replace more radical and demanding ethical imperatives.

The Use and Abuse of Religion

The foregoing descriptions of popularly held beliefs in the evangelical and liberal traditions are certainly not accurate in every detail. Nevertheless, as characterizations, I think they are sufficiently accurate and familiar to indicate those elements in both traditions that contribute to indifference. Both traditions contain many points that impede effective social ethics. Each of these points represents a grain of truth that, when carried to the extreme, becomes false.

It is true, for example, that we are spiritual creatures. But if we are defined as spiritual creatures exclusively, without legitimate corporal needs, then the doctrine about our spiritual nature distorts the Christian message and becomes demonstrably false. Similarly, it is true that we are individuals, responsible before God for our actions. We are, however, also social creatures and members of communities. To accept the first proposition while denying the second is again, I think, categorically false. From a different, more liberal perspective, it is arguably the case that individual efforts to alleviate social problems represent only a temporary, "Band-Aid" approach. Such a perspective, however, is again false if it is used to deny individual responsibility and obligations, however small, local, and unsystematic they may be.

Taken in isolation, none of the propositions we have reviewed is entirely false. A proposition becomes false only when it is used to dismiss our obligations and responsibilities. What do we tell ourselves in excusing our indifference? What categories of thought and perception permit us to remain blind to the problems? Whenever we use the doctrines of dualism and individualism, whenever we perceive the church and our participation in community as optional, whenever we misuse the Bible, we falsify the theological traditions, whether liberal or evangelical, to which we are heirs. Rather than confronting indifference, these falsified traditions support and legitimate our indifference in a way that makes it even more recalcitrant. Because of our unwitting beliefs about the church, the Bible, individualism, and the division between body and spirit, we are impeded either in seeing or in acknowledging our moral imperatives.

CHAPTER FOUR

Popular Culture:
The Stories of Indifference

The tendency to indifference displayed by individuals is reinforced by a corresponding tendency embedded in a culture. The books and movies, the arts and sports, the dance and music, the newspapers and magazines that collectively constitute a culture (especially a popular culture) make up a moral universe as well. In particular, certain stories extant within a culture emerge to become reference points for our moral compasses, embodying for us our deepest and often only half-perceived aspirations and values.

Two such stories repeatedly frame the American experience: the story of success, exemplified by the entrepreneur ascending from rags to riches; and the story of the lone, self-reliant hero best and most classically expressed by the American cowboy. However simplistic or incredible their stories may seem on the surface, the stylized struggles and triumphs of the entrepreneur and the cowboy nevertheless continue to define and inspire their cultural benefactors.

The academic study of mythology and, more recently, of ethics demonstrates the power of stories to inform the way we see and structure experience, including our moral experience. Life imitates art (most powerfully when that imitation is neither perceived nor acknowledged) whenever we model our perception and behavior on the stories current in a culture. In American culture, the biblical story of the exodus served to inspire moral commitment and sacrifice during the civil rights struggle just as, in another era, the story of the Alamo inspired a more dubious commitment to national sovereignty. Obverse to the commitments inspired by the stories of the Alamo and the exodus, however, are the stories in our culture—the stories of the entrepreneur and the cowboy—that serve to reinforce moral indifference. If indifference, as well as commitment, can be attributed to the artful models and symbols expressed by and contained within stories, then freedom to act on behalf of others requires first freeing ourselves from the narratives that reinforce our deep-seated propensity for moral indifference.

First, then, I will review the stories of the cowboy and the entrepreneur, the classic American stories first formulated during the nineteenth century. Next I will turn to what is, perhaps, the pre-eminent twentieth-century story, the story that there is no story. If, as recent scholarship persuasively argues, narratives are an essential ingredient for coherent moral action, then the abandonment of stories leads to an indifference by default. In a world without narrative, indifference is not attributable to wrong action but to a lack of coherent, narrated action. In such a world, ethics is literally unaccountable. The story of having no story, because it contributes directly to an inability to act, is an exemplary narrative of absences and thus an important moment in our reflections.

Through Pluck
and Persistence

The story of the entrepreneur is the story of success. Classically, a poor, usually rural, boy moves to the city and there—unaided by anything but his own initiative, hard work, pluck, and persistence—overcomes obstacle after obstacle until success is his. Horatio Alger built his career around telling and retelling the success stories of such characters as Plucky Pete, Tattered Tom, and Lightning Luke in more than 130 novels. The veracity of Alger's fictionalized accounts was documented in the real-life stories from the Gilded Age in which he wrote and the decades following it—success stories of men such as Thomas Edison, Henry Ford, and John D. Rockefeller. The man (and classically it was a man) most admired and lionized in America is the one depicted by Alger, not the man who inherits his wealth or position, but the self-made man who starts with nothing and—through pluck, persistence, and cleverness—ends in the opulence of a Biltmore House. In our own day, Lee Iacocca is admired not simply because he is the head of Chrysler Corporation but because he succeeded in turning a failing company into an example of its own slogan, "The pride is back."

The rags-to-riches motif associated with Horatio Alger may be expressed in a variety of ways. Politically, it may mean the distance from a log cabin to the White House. In the arts and professions, it may mean the distance from obscurity and ridicule to recognition and honors. In sports, it may mean overcoming limitation and a lack of innate talent to become a superstar. The widespread acceptance of the success story, regardless of the specific context, may be attributed to its ability to incorporate the three fundamental motifs of growth, fairness, and objectivity.

Growth and Progress. The movement from rags to riches is a movement of growth and progress. Growth, as one observer has noted, "is the oldest, most powerful and encompassing" metaphor in Western thought. Like growth, the story of success gives to experience purpose and direction. Life is not random, static, or cyclic; on the contrary, it moves in a single, cumulative direction. Life is a progression; it goes from beginning to end, from small to large. My expectations and sense of self-esteem are defined by the rate at which I am moving forward. If I am advancing in my career, if I am steadily climbing the ladder of success, then I am content and hopeful. If, on the other hand, I am not advancing at work, if I am stuck (the telling word) in my job or my marriage, then I am discontented and burdened with a vague feeling of failure and disappointment. The presumption of growth and progressive movement defines how we see and evaluate both ourselves and others.

The simple story of growth and progress is a subtle lesson in indifference, in at least two respects. First, the prospect of growth and progress implies that poverty is temporary. Poor living conditions and an inadequate education represent temporary beginning points from which I can progress. Plucky Pete started out poor and unsophisticated, but look where he ended up! Henry Ford began as a night foreman but became one of America's greatest industrialists. Poverty is tolerable, both for the poor and the nonpoor alike, whenever it is seen as a challenge and not as a recalcitrant, permanent condition. Poverty is acceptable precisely because it can be left behind. Immigrants came to America with only the shirts on their backs, but inspired by the prospect of success they gradually moved from the ghettos into the mainstream of American life. The Kennedys, for example, began as Irish immigrants and bootleggers. If I or others can move beyond poverty, as many demonstrably have, then I can afford to be indifferent to its existence and causes. Rich and poor alike can afford to ignore present conditions because the story of success directs our attention to the future. Attentive to a future prospect of success, we remain indifferent to present conditions of need.

The second way the story of success informs indifference involves our own response to moral action. Moral action often displays a frustrating lack of tangible progress. Demonstrations against nuclear weapons and programs to aid the homeless or to end hunger frequently seem both fruitless and unending. Placed within the context of a story that measures success by progress, the question, What can one person do? receives a dishearteningly empty response. Despite the efforts and good intentions of people, the nuclear arms race continues unabated and thousands die every day from easily preventable diseases. Schooled on a presumption of cumulative advancement, the apparent lack of demonstrable progress frequently associated with moral action leads to frustration, discouragement, and a sense of failure. When we are confronted by moral efforts that seemingly fail to "progress," an indifference either of hopelessness or exhaustion soon follows.

Fairness.   The story of success is a story of equal opportunity. Fairness legitimizes the discrepancy that always emerges between the successful and those who fail. Most often, and most aptly, the story of success is compared to a footrace. The analogy of the footrace suggests that each contestant has an equal start and that, second, no contestant is severely handicapped or disadvantaged. At least at the start, everyone has an equal chance of winning the race. Furthermore, once the race has begun, each participant is subject to the same rules and obstacles. Everyone runs the same distance, beneath the same sun. If, in the end, a clear winner emerges, he or she does so because of individual merit. The distinction between winner and loser is an earned inequality and thus acceptable. The winner deserves the spoils and privileges of victory because he or she has trained harder, run faster, and "paid the price" of success.

Strictly interpreted, the analogy of a footrace suggests that only one person (or at least a limited number of persons) can be a winner. If there can be only a limited number of winners, then a latecomer to the race might be at an unfair disadvantage. In order to avoid this potential source of unfairness, the story of success proclaims that everyone can be a winner. Horace Greeley's advice to "go west" was predicated on the belief that "success is within the reach of everyone who will truly and boldly seek it." In an environment of limitless resources and opportunity, success is never at the expense of someone else. In contrast to the Marxist story of revolution, success does not mean the inevitable suppression or exploitation of the losers. My success does not depend on someone else's failure; on the contrary, there is more than enough success to go around for all of those who are willing to work steadfastly to achieve it.

The fairness inherent within the success story permits a studied indifference toward the less fortunate. If everyone begins the race equally, then both victory and defeat are equally merited. Success or failure rests entirely with the individual; because success is earned, the successful individual has a right to enjoy his or her success without guilt. Perhaps the most ironic aspect of the success story is this: It persuades most of the participants to accept and to become good losers. Losers, as well as winners, can be "good" (indifferent to the outcome) because the story of success both guarantees fairness of opportunity and looks expectantly forward to another day.

The story of success ignores what, in more reflective moments, may be obvious. We do not all start the race equally; some are more intelligent or gifted than others, some come from more supportive and loving families, some have more economic and social advantages. People succeed because of who they know or just plain luck, whereas many fail because they are treated unfairly and unjustly. The race is, as Ecclesiastes reminds us, not always to the swift. Because the story of success ignores the factors—especially the social factors—contributing to unfairness, we tend to do likewise. Secure in the knowledge that the story of success more or less reflects things as they are, that the distance between my life and the life of the poor is merited and earned rather than accidental and arbitrary, I can remain comfortably indifferent toward the needs of others. There may be vast differences between my life and those of the working poor, but the discrepancy in itself does not constitute a problem. The story of success is legitimized because everyone has an equal opportunity to succeed, if not today then tomorrow. Both the winners and the losers merit their level of success.

Objectivity. Success means many things to many people, but in America success has most often meant money. Assessing the success of someone is as easy and objective as counting the assets in his or her stock portfolio. Success, particularly financial success, provides a common denominator, a democratic, universal, and insistently anti-metaphysical yardstick for determining merit. Especially in a socially and geographically mobile society like America, financial status replaces the more traditional forms of status afforded by family, place, or profession. Go anywhere, do anything, it doesn't matter. I can still judge myself and others according to the universal and objective standard of wealth.

Compared to the financial standard of success, more subjective standards—including commitment to intangible moral values—seem vague, parochial, or elitist. Who is to say that commitment to the poor is more noble than being president of Exxon? Who is to say that commitment to helping a friend is any more important than staying late at work to complete a project, or that commitment to a career is less important than participating in the PTA? In contrast to an objective financial standard, appeals to less tangible values, rewards, or achievements are less than persuasive. The intangible commitments and rewards of community participation, honesty, and humility seem less substantial, less real somehow, than those that can be objectively counted. Commitment to an objective, democratic standard serves to undermine commitment to the less measurable rewards of moral action.

The objectivity of the success story contains one additional corollary: The objective standard has no inherent limits. If more is better, then even more is even better. No mechanism for asking when enough is enough is present; as a consequence, there is an implied moral imperative for limitless growth. The doctrine that "more is better" drives the motif of growth and progress continuously, whatever the context. The limitlessness of the objective standard defines the technological imperative to build "better" missile systems, to extend life indefinitely, and to participate in unconstrained consumerism. Without limits, the map of moral action lacks coordinates, a boundary beyond which continued growth and progress are inappropriate.

Success.   The story of success incorporates the stories of growth, fairness, and objective measurement. Fairness and objectivity serve to legitimate and authenticate the veracity of the core growth motif inherent in the story of success. Whatever qualifications and reservations we may have toward these stories in more reflective moments, they are nevertheless muted by the continuing ability of the stories to capture and thus inform our attention.

The story of success informs our expectations and aspirations and provides a moral compass to our moral bearings. For the less fortunate, the story that progress is possible—that opportunity awaits and that one is judged by financial success and not racial or social beginnings—has and continues to inspire, and rightly so. For those who have achieved a measure of success, however, the story serves the function of reassuring us that the story is true, that poverty is temporary, that the competition for success is fair and equitable, and that there is an objective standard by which our actions can be judged. For both winners and losers, the story of success provides structure and direction. The dark side of the story, however, is that it fosters moral indifference to the recalcitrance of need, the injustice of luck and environment, and the limitlessness of greed. Indifference is complementary to our commitment to the story of success. Freedom from indifference requires freeing ourselves from the narrative of success that informs and expresses our deep-seated tendency toward moral indifference.

The American Cowboy

The second story informing American experience is the story of the lone, self-reliant hero, best and most classically expressed in the legend of the American cowboy. The cowboy's story (and the stories of his more contemporary incarnations—whether as surgeon, starship commander, or police officer) follows the simple formula articulated by Robert Jewett: "A community in a harmonious paradise is threatened by evil: normal institutions fail to contend with this threat: a selfless superhero emerges to renounce temptations and carry out the redemptive task: aided by fate, his decisive victory restores the community to its paradisal condition: the superhero then recedes into obscurity."

Reduced to its formulalike essentials, the story of the cowboy has three interrelated parts: a setting, a statement concerning the nature and origins of evil, and a narrative explanation about how evil can be overcome. In the following three sections, I briefly describe each of these components in order to demonstrate how they reinforce our deep-seated propensity for moral indifference.

The Setting. The cowboy's story is played out in infinite variety, but always it is played out in the West. The West (that period in American history that became an indigenous mythology) is not limited to the Great Plains and southwestern deserts of America; the West refers to any frontier, whether it occurs in Texas or the reaches of space or a hospital. As a genre of literature and television entertainment, the classic Western may fade in popularity; but as a frontier, the appeal of the West remains universal. A frontier marks the border between civilization and wilderness, a confrontation between good and evil, life and death, whenever and wherever it may occur. Any narrative that contains the stark, dualistic confrontations typified by the cowboy's story is, by definition, in the lineage of the classic Western. In real life, the division between good and evil is not always clear but, when viewed through the perspective of the Western, choices are both clear-cut and decisive.

The dualistic confrontation endemic to the Western creates an inherent sense of drama and excitement. The story of the cowboy is a story of challenge and confrontation, of dramatic action and struggle. It is not a story of growth or discovery or revolution. The Western depicts, indeed, invites, moments of crisis and combat. Because the contrasts are clear and simple, the victory of one side over the other is important. Loyalties in such conflicts are never ambiguous or divided. One observer of popular culture has noted that the ritual of victory is a confirmation of America's deepest values. When the sheriff straps on his gun, everyone knows that something exciting and important is about to happen.

The Western setting contributes to indifference in at least two ways. First, accustomed to the clear, unambiguous choices presented in a Western, we easily become frustrated with complexity. Ethical choices between abortion and the right of women to have control of their own bodies, for example, are frequently hard choices with equally ambiguous outcomes. The ambiguity of such choices creates the anxiety and uncertainty that Niebuhr identified as one of the root causes of indifference. As a result, the dualistic framework exemplified by the Western reinforces our inherent tendency to accept the simple analysis and decisive solution. Tutored by the Western, we expect an unambiguous solution (victory), and when one is not immediately forthcoming, we tend to abandon the ambiguity of moral decision altogether.

A second way in which the Western contributes to moral indifference involves its emphasis on the spectacular confrontations between good and evil. Attentive to the excitement of the dramatic confrontation, our sensibilities are correspondingly less attentive to the more subtle, less decisive dramas of day-to-day living. Like the townspeople depicted in the Western itself, we wait passively until something big and exciting captures our attention, all the while ignoring the incremental acts and movements that constitute both good and ill. Too easily, we equate the important with the dramatic. This may be seen in issues of health care. Research and foundational support flows toward dramatic programs such as heart transplants, rather than routine, less dramatic programs such as immunization and school lunch programs. More money is spent on lung cancer than on preventing people from smoking. Medicare pays for organ transplants, yet 20 percent of American schoolchildren are not immunized against polio. Addicted to the crisis mentality of the Western, we are correspondingly less attentive (indifferent) to the incremental changes in diet and life-style that could significantly reduce incidents of cancer and stroke. Bewitched by the spectacle of emergency aid for victims of floods and famine, we do not see or are less attentive to the factors that create environmental strain and failure. In short, we are like the Western's townspeople, who are passive before the outlaw rides into town. The similarity between the passivity of the townspeople before the outlaw rides into town and our own passivity before moral imperatives reflects the complacency of those schooled on the narrative of the cowboy.

The Source and Nature of Evil. The indifference inherent in the crisis-filled, dualistic setting of the Western is reinforced by the Western's understanding of evil. Evil is not indigenous to the town, but comes as an incursion from outside. A Western begins when a villain wearing a black hat rides into a sleepy, complacent town. The villain's appearance is sudden, unexpected, and—we are led to believe—wholly undeserved. The town is not responsible for evil; indeed, the choice of the villain to ride into one town rather than another seems entirely arbitrary. Because they are isolated in the West, the townspeople are more vulnerable to evil than most, but that vulnerability does not compromise their essential innocence. The confrontation between good and evil depicted in a Western is initiated by the incursion of evil; apart from that initiative, the townspeople remain complacent and seemingly innocent, like Eve before the appearance of the snake.

In addition to being external, from a source outside the community, evil is also understood to be recalcitrant. The villain is not confused or misguided; on the contrary, he is—in contrast to the corresponding innocence of the townspeople—beyond redemption and evil to the core. The story presents a titanic struggle between pure good and pure evil. From the first moments of the drama, it is clear that there can be no compromise or peaceful solution to the threat that rides into town; the villain will not wake up one morning and, realizing the evil of his ways, ask forgiveness. Unrepentant to the end, the villain's challenge to the town can have only one, typically violent, outcome.

The Western's understanding that evil is both external and recalcitrant contributes to indifference in two ways. First, by locating the source of evil outside the community, the Western reinforces the status quo and presumed innocence of the community. If evil is outside the community, then there is no necessity for the townspeople to acknowledge their participation or complicity in evil. If the town is not responsible for evil, then there is no call for self-examination, criticism, or reform. If the community is essentially good, then it is permitted to wait passively until it must react to evil.

In our own day, this same mentality surrounds the issue of unemployment. The presumed innocence of the community permits us to attribute poverty to laziness and poor work habits, rather than to factors indigenous in our communities. If the evils of unemployment and poverty simply "arrive" without provocation or cause like the man in the black hat, then we are permitted to remain indifferent to how our participation in failing educational and economic policies contributes to these evils. Reassured by a pattern established by the Western, the middle class sees itself as an innocent community under siege and thus fails to acknowledge its own responsibility for the creation of a permanent underclass.

Second, the Western encourages indifference by depicting evil as recalcitrant. If evil is inherent, we are released from the responsibility of trying to discern the causes of evil; our only responsibility is to defend our interests and to repel the incursion. Thus, in the formulation of foreign policy, we define our policy in Central America in light of the threat of communism rather than in light of poverty. Opponents to abortion can be assured that what they oppose is inherently evil, without taking account of the social and psychological conditions that lead to unwanted pregnancies and abortion. If evil is evil, if what we oppose is finally not like us, then we are justified in treating opponents in any way that is expedient. No effort at understanding or conversion is possible or necessary. Defeating the enemy is our only responsibility.

The Solution to Evil.   The third element of the cowboy story that contributes to indifference is associated with the cowboy himself. The cowboy is distinguished by both his hero status and the means he typically employs for combating the threat of evil. The cowboy hero emerges from a background of ordinariness. When the man with the black hat rides into town, the townspeople are oddly but persistently passive. Presumedly, the townspeople are collectively capable of defending themselves against a small band of desperadoes. The townspeople could organize themselves into a militia; they could rally around a slogan such as "united we stand, divided we fall," but they do not. Bandits, as William James once remarked, have always relied on the fact that those being robbed lack the faith to join collectively and concurrently in defending themselves. The passivity of the townspeople, their inability to act, makes the emergence of the hero necessary. In the typical Western, only the hero stands between the town and chaos. Incapable of helping themselves, the townspeople wait for a redeemer hero who will act on their behalf.

The emergence of a redeemer hero signals the arrival of someone extraordinary and special. The hero acts to save the townspeople, but he is clearly not one of them. Often of unknown lineage, almost never a native of the town, the hero is *in* but not *of* this world. The cowboy is a hero precisely because he possesses more skill, courage, initiative, and luck than the rest of us. The figure of the hero stands against, and is defined by, the ordinariness of the townspeople. Where they are passive, he is active; where they are indecisive and vulnerable, he is decisive and strong; where they are waiting for redemption, for someone else to save them, he assumes responsibility and takes matters into his own hands.

The cowboy is distinguished by his hero status, but he is also distinguished by the means he employs for combating evil. In contrast to the ineffectiveness of the townspeople, the hero (normally through violence and against all odds) acts decisively and alone—or with a few companions—to repel evil. The hero is not a politician or a bureaucrat. Befitting his status as an outsider, he does not become involved with the entanglements and compromises of the community. His actions are swift, unencumbered, and dramatic, rather than systematic and deliberate. Both the townspeople themselves and their laws are ineffective in combating evil; indeed, precisely the ineffectiveness of the normal, ordinary institutions has made the hero's emergence necessary. Not surprisingly, the hero must go outside the law in order to preserve the community. Ironically, the community is thus saved through nondemocratic means. The community is redeemed not through community action, but through the extraordinary efforts of an individual.

Because evil is recalcitrant, the hero's defeat of evil must be unconditional. The hero does not argue with evil, try to understand its causes, or rely on civil debate and persuasion. On the contrary, the hero acts decisively through violence to a sudden, conclusive end. Violence guarantees that the confrontation between good and evil will be swift and clean. The combat of the cowboy is not a form of guerrilla warfare where victories and goals are excessively political and ambiguous. On the contrary, the cowboy avoids the frustration of incremental reform or political compromise by evoking a dramatic, "heroic" resolution.

The cowboy's special status and method of combating evil contribute to social indifference by undermining the legitimacy of collective, institutional action by ordinary citizens. Schooled in the expectation that redemption arrives in the form of an extraordinary hero, the more routine actions of ordinary citizens are either not seen or devalued. If redemption, like evil, is not indigenous to the community, ordinary citizens are permitted to remain expectantly passive. Adoration of the hero lessens the status of ordinary people and their ability to act. Similarly, tutored in the apolitical, noninstitutional means the hero employs, we are less likely to see or acknowledge the compromises and incremental advances of community-wide action. Accustomed to decisive action, to the ability to get things done through direct means, we are frustrated with the slow, indecisive results of the political process, with committees, and the limitations of voluntary associations. In simplest terms, the example of the cowboy trains us to expect that problems will be resolved by extraordinary people using extraordinary means in a way that undermines our reliance on the more ordinary, if less spectacular, acts of common citizens. As a result, we are enamored by Hands Across America and the spectacles of Live Aid concerts, rather than the more humble works performed by the Heifer Project or Bread for the World. Moral action is often more routine and ordinary than spectacular. Informed by the story of the cowboy, however, we fail to see the day-in, day-out nature of moral action in the absence of the spectacular or a redeeming hero. "What can *we* do to change things?" is the slogan of those nurtured on the story of the cowboy.

The Subtle Power of Stories.   The story of the cowboy structures the way we perceive and evaluate our moral universe. Tutored in this narrative, we define evil as being outside our community and responsibility. Poverty is a problem that elicits a call for charity rather than justice, for emergency, reactionary aid rather than social reform. Addicted to the dramatic and the spectacular, attention is captured by big events in South Africa or Nicaragua rather than the less dramatic but more insidious forms of injustice closer to home. Unable to directly participate in the "major moral confrontations of our times," we remain indifferent to the moral issues facing our local neighborhoods and institutions. Always expectant and bewitched by the necessity for a leader, a redeemer hero who can bring recognition and status to an issue, we ignore our own moral capacities for good.

Convinced that the Soviets or abortionists are recalcitrantly evil, our indifference to their perspective is legitimized. Dismayed by the inefficiency of the justice system (including the tax codes), our reliance on community processes such as voting is undermined. Conditioned to expect a simple division between right and wrong, and a quick, decisive victory of one over the other, we are frustrated with complexity and ambiguity.

People are not simply indifferent, as in a vacuum. They are indifferent because of their commitments to stories that structure and reinforce indifference. No story of the cowboy or entrepreneur incorporates all of the elements discussed or, for that matter, would anyone admit their influence. There is no incontestable instance of how such stories inform moral perception and behavior. Nevertheless, the suggestion remains that, collectively and subliminally, the motifs popularized and exemplified by the entrepreneur and the cowboy provide the bits and pieces, the "fragments shored against our ruins," with which indifference is legitimized. Whenever commitments are uncomfortable or inconvenient, we rely on such narratives to justify our indifference. Comforted by the familiar patterns they express and perpetuate, we are reassured in our complacency in a way that undermines our ability to recognize that a moral problem exists. To free ourselves from indifference, it is first necessary to free ourselves from the stories that reinforce our propensity for moral indifference.

The Story of Having No Story

Study of the cowboy and the entrepreneur is predicated on the belief that stories provide examples and symbols through and by means of which we give shape, direction, and meaning to our lives, both individually and collectively. Michael Novak has suggested the specific relationship between stories and ethics by saying that, like no other method, stories are capable of linking or tying together a person's actions in a sequence. Purposeful action and moral commitment invariably describe a story. Moral action means living out one story rather than another—the story of one neighbor helping another, rather than the story of everyone being out for himself or herself alone.

The importance of stories to ethics implies a negative corollary that Novak himself recognized. If stories are a necessary means of giving shape to the moral life, then the absence of stories means the absence of a morally coherent life. Apart from an implicit story, action seems pointless. "Without the narrative unity of a story," Novak writes, "life becomes increasingly listless and inactive," or, in the terms of our discussion, indifferent. Complementing the story of the cowboy and entrepreneur is the story of having no story. Storylessness is itself a story, one that, as we will see, is especially appropriate to moral indifference.

The Refusal to Tell a Story.   An attempt to prove the absence of stories and the moral consequences of that absence confronts the philosophical caution regarding the difficulty of proving a negative. Perhaps in lieu of such proof, then, a brief review of contemporary literature's refusal to tell a story will have to suffice. In the course of that review, I want to examine the nature and reasons for that refusal, as well as to reflect briefly on the significance of that refusal for moral commitments.

More than one observer has noted that the interest in stories among theologians and ethicists comes at a time when the literary community itself is abandoning conventional narratives. Fictional works such as Nabokov's *Pale Fire* or Borges's *Labyrinths* and non-fictional works such as George Aichele's *The Limits of Story* challenge conventional storytelling. More than the story of the cowboy or the entrepreneur, the story of having no story is, according to the scholar Nathan Scott, "an expression of the post-narrative, post-modern period style *most characteristic* of our age" (emphasis mine).

The refusal or inability of contemporary literature to tell a story is exemplified by the work of Samuel Beckett. The disintegration of narrative in the literary career of Beckett, culminating in the incessant ramblings of *Waiting for Godot* and *The Unnameable,* is traced in Ted Estes's seminal essay on "The Inenarrable Contraption: Reflections on the Metaphor of Story." Estes concludes that emptied of narrative structure altogether, the protagonists of Beckett's stories "typically depart with uncertain intentions, journey aimlessly, and seldom return. . . . Many of his characters fail to perceive even the possibility for imposing upon or discovering within their experience a coherently integrated structure which we call 'plot.' "

Estes attributes Beckett's refusal to tell a story to four factors. First, the refusal to form a story is thought to be truer to real life. If life is experienced or conceived to be disconnected, fragmentary, or fleeting, if all we have is what we live from moment to moment, then the structure and order provided by narrative is a falsification or distortion of that phenomenological experience. Stories are comfortable and reassuring; we like to have a sense that there is a beginning "once upon a time" and an ending "happily ever after." The reassurance of order, the human propensity or "rage for order," however, may be a means of denying the true chaos all around us. In contrast to a fictive order, the apparent chaos of the story that has no story may actually expose us to the real world in a way not possible in the selective, intentional structure of conventional narrative.

The second reason Beckett refuses to tell a story involves (according to Estes) a fidelity to finitude. The ability to narrate a story from beginning to end, to discern a progression or digression, to order by an act of causal, logical, or teleological imagination, implies a "breadth of perspective" that Beckett's characters are incapable of achieving. The ability to link one action with another, to go from here to there, either to anticipate or to remember, implies a minimum degree of transcendence and confidence in the future. Beckett's characters are permeated by the experience of failure, a failure precisely to gain sufficient transcendence to order their lives into any coherent pattern. What one person sees as failure, however, another interprets as success. The failure to gain perspective concurrently represents a fidelity to the momentary, to the contingencies and indeterminacies of the here and now. In an era characterized by the death of God, all forms of transcendence, even the human forms of transcendence represented by memory and expectation, seem false and artificial.

According to Estes, Beckett's refusal to tell a story is attributable thirdly to the privatization of experience. Stories not only give order and coherence to individual experience; they also provide a public, shared means of expression. The conventions of beginning and end, of one thing coming after and leading to the next, are public in nature; they provide a common basis from which we can communicate our experiences. As one descends into the self, however, as in a dream, conventions of time and space disintegrate and become less meaningful. If one presumes that this private self is more real than the public realm, that essentially we are alone in this world, then the requirement to integrate experience according to the space and time conventions embodied by narrative is both unnecessary and a violation of one's truest experience. In a completely private world, the public conventional self, the self that is literally accountable, disintegrates into a stream of images, fragments, and private symbols.

A fourth, and final, reason for refusing to tell a story involves inaction in an otherwise meaningless world. Story is inseparable from purposive action; a story is, as Estes reminds us, an "implicit affirmation that something of significance has been done by someone." Actions speak louder than words precisely because actions reveal that to which we are committed. In this sense, ethics is a display of theology. If we do not think one action is better than another or that one state of affairs is better than another, then purposeful action, action that begins at one point and deliberately ends at another, is undermined. Without purpose, action becomes more and more problematic and random; there is no reason, beyond impulse, for doing one thing rather than another. There is no standard with which to judge good from evil.

The refusal to tell a story expresses a commitment to a certain view of reality. If reality is chaotic and episodic, if persons are incapable of at least a minimum degree of transcendence, if who we are is defined exclusively by the here and now or by what we hold in private, if one thing is no more important than another, then the refusal to impose the artificial structure of a story is an act of honesty and courage. Storyless people bravely face contingencies without the reassurance of infantile stories and myths. At the same time, however, they undermine the narrative basis of moral action and thus encourage indifference.

The Storyless Story and Ethics. The story of having no story reflects an environment hostile to both stories and moral commitment. Dismissed by some as elitist, the storyless stories of Beckett may nevertheless express the storylessness in which most of us live. What are the stories through which we give shape and meaning to our lives? To what extent, when such stories become inconvenient, are we committed to them? Trust in stories has waned ever since they were dismissed by the Enlightenment as primitive and nonrational. Few of the traditional cultural stories we have inherited succeed in sustaining our commitments. Confronted by a variety of conflicting stories, no single story can command our allegiance. Morally, not to have any story to live out is to experience nothingness, the primal "formlessness of human life below the threshold of narrative structuring." Estes attributes Beckett's refusal to tell a story to an a priori nihilism in a way that suggests the priority of philosophy over story. From a perspective that assumes the priority of stories over philosophy, however, nihilism may itself be attributable to the lack of any culturally sustaining stories. We are not storyless because we are nihilistic; we are nihilistic because we are storyless. Bewitched by the story of having no story, we hold no narrative structure or coherence to sustain moral commitment.

Consider for a moment absence and its effects. Traditionally, stories were related to moral commitment in at least two ways. First, stories of heroes and saints were examples in comparison to which we found our own stories wanting. Inspired by the story of those who sacrificed their lives for others, our own protestations concerning the inconvenience of helping others were undermined. Second, stories, specifically "religious" stories, served in legitimizing our actions. We were willing to sacrifice ourselves because the myths of "heaven and hell" and of simply being a "good" person legitimized moral action. In contrast to these two uses of story, how does the story of having no story reinforce moral commitment when moral commitment becomes inconvenient? The inability to provide an adequate answer to that question is a telling remark on how the story of having no story is a narrative particularly appropriate to indifference.

The stories of the entrepreneur and the cowboy contribute to indifference by diverting attention from moral commitment. Intent on racing toward riches, we neglect the ways in which life can be unjust. Attentive to the heroic skills of the cowboy, we too easily discount our own, less dramatic abilities to affect change. Like all myths, the mythic stories of the cowboy and the entrepreneur educate us to the reality they present. Seen through the lens of the cowboy, for example, the source of evil is always outside our communities. We do not decide about this; we simply understand that "it's just the way things are; it's just the way we see things." The myth precludes other possibilities as long as we live within its purview or spell. Commitment to ethics requires debunking those myths of indifference that nurture our indifference.

If myths of indifference succeed for some in sustaining moral indifference by diverting our attention elsewhere, then the myth of having no myths (the story of having no story) radically undermines the basis of moral action for others. We have said that moral commitment often requires a deliberate effort to debunk the myths of indifference. In contrast, the story of having no story requires a movement in the opposite direction, a rediscovery or invention of morally compelling stories. Of the two tasks, the debunking task is surely the easier, for it is not entirely clear how one goes about discovering or inventing a functional myth. Certainly, one can begin the task by debunking the story of having no story itself, by relativizing the relativizers as Peter Berger once wrote, but after that the course is not clear. Various authors have expressed the widespread desire to move beyond the storyless modern mind to a postmodern consciousness, but how that cultural movement can be accomplished is uncertain. Until it is accomplished, however, the story of having no story is a black hole in the midst of which moral commitment is improbable and sporadic. Beckett's refusal to tell a story reflects a fragmented, imminent, nihilistic, and private existence endemic to indifference and the twentieth century. The moral life, after all, is inseparable from a commitment to continuity, transcendence, values, and the public realm inherent in a storied life.

CHAPTER FIVE

Public Life:
The Ideology of Indifference

In chapters 3 and 4 we reviewed how, in the realms of popular theology and culture, certain stories and concepts contribute to moral indifference. We saw, for example, how the rags-to-riches story supports indifference by reassuring us that poverty is temporary and amenable to hard work. In this chapter we will examine how the concepts and stories associated with the notion of freedom contribute to moral indifference in the political realm. As Americans living in the modern world, we accept a host of unexamined notions about what the world is like, how we should live in it, and the way we should act toward one another. Whenever concepts and stories function mythically by informing our perception and behavior in the public realm, they become ideologies. In many instances, indifference to social ethics is attributable to our commitment to what may be termed "ideologies of indifference." Debunking these ideologies is prelude to moral commitment in the public realm.

Shortly, we will look at the specific impediments to moral commitment we have inherited as heirs to the long and familiar history of freedom. Before turning to this particular history, however, we need to consider how concepts function in general. How do concepts work, and what is their importance to moral indifference and commitment?

Ideology: The Mythology
of Concepts

Conventionally, ethics has centered its discussion of concepts on moral rules and propositions. The familiar "you shall nots" are a convenient example. "You shall not kill" provokes a discussion about the concept of killing: How is the concept delimited and to what situations does it apply? Such considerations are largely deliberate and self-conscious exercises, appropriately abstracted from immediate contexts.

Before such deliberate exercises, however, concepts—like stories—provide subtle frameworks that orient us in the world in ways that are less visible and thus more powerful than their more self-consciously held counterparts. Concepts simplify and provide unity to otherwise diverse and complex experiences. The concept of oppression, for example, gives shape and meaning to the poverty experienced by peoples of the third world. How is poverty to be seen or interpreted? Is poverty simply bad luck? Is it attributable to laziness or a lack of character? Is it simply a case of underdevelopment, or is it due to the deliberate oppression and exploitation of one nation over another?

One's moral apprehension and response to poverty are informed by the concept through which it is interpreted. If people are poor because they lack initiative, then they must bear responsibility for their condition. If, however, they are poor because they are victims of deliberate oppression, then they may legitimately seek ways to depose, through revolution perhaps, their oppressors. The concept of oppression permits people to see themselves in a different light; it is one thing to be poor because of misfortune, but quite another thing altogether to be poor because of the deliberate, calculated malevolence of others. Variously used by peoples of the third world, by workers in labor disputes, by women, and by self-defined "victims" of racial and religious discrimination, the category of oppression is an exemplary instance of how concepts supply moral bearings to otherwise morally chartless situations.

Whenever concepts are used to interpret experience, whenever they orient understanding, behavior, or attitude, they assume a mythical function. Mythical concepts come to light when we are unable easily to provide a synonym or substitute expression. Mythical concepts signal an end to discussion. Like archetypal myths, archetypal concepts are irreplaceable and have a life of their own. The concepts of justice or truth or equality convey something greater than any specific instance or story. We can tell numerous stories of how people have gone from rags to riches, but no collection of such stories fully encompasses the concept of opportunity. Concepts and stories are mythically complementary. Concepts simplify and provide unity to the narrative diversity of stories, just as stories provide richness and substance to more abstract concepts. Functionally concepts, working in conjunction with stories, are mythical in nature.

Unlike stories, concepts are commonly thought to be the preserve of academics and philosophers. An acknowledgment that concepts function mythically by influencing our stance toward both the world and others means that they are the providence of common folk as well as intellectuals. It is not necessary to their effectiveness that we hold such concepts self-consciously, nor is it important that we know a concept's origin and lineage. On the contrary, the power of concepts, like the power of stories, frequently depends on invisibility. Often unwittingly, each of us practices and lives out a host of unexamined concepts daily—as Mortimer Adler has convincingly demonstrated in *Six Great Ideas* and *Ten Philosophical Mistakes*. Our concepts, as well as our experience and stories, predispose us to act in one way rather than in another, to see and interpret from a particular vantage point. If, to quote the title of a book by Joseph Campbell, there are *Myths to Live By*, no less a claim can be made for concepts.

The importance of concepts in shaping perception and action suggests their role in encouraging either moral commitment or moral indifference. On the one hand, a concept such as solidarity or self-sacrifice may encourage us to work on behalf of others, and, on the other hand, a concept of individualism or personal success may lead to an exclusive concern for self-aggrandizing behavior and indifference to social ethics. In the latter instance, the indifference indigenous to individualism and success is undermined by debunking the concept of the self-sufficient, autonomous individual. Debunking the concept of individualism, like debunking the narrative of rags to riches, means transforming the given, the accepted, and the taken-for-granted into a matter of deliberate, self-conscious choice and decision. Although self-conscious choice is not a guarantee of commitment, it is a first step in instances where we are beguiled by a concept of indifference. Indifference is supported by concepts as well as stories; undermining those concepts through a technique of debunking is an important means for shifting our allegiances from those "ideologies of indifference" to moral commitment.

From Freedom to Indifference

In common parlance, freedom means the absence of restraint, obstacles, or coercion. To be free is to be without restriction, compulsion, or obligation. "Free as a bird," "do as you please"—such phrases express a desire to manage our lives without outside restriction or interference. Advertisers successfully appeal to this deep-seated archetypal search for freedom, whether it is the freedom of the open road, the freedom from bad breath, or the freedom from sexual inhibition. Our nation celebrates freedom every Fourth of July and proclaims the freedoms guaranteed by the Constitution. Individually, each of us carries personal associations with the notion of freedom. We yearn for freedom from the constraints of a job, a marriage, the responsibility of children, illness, a psychological neurosis, cultural mores, and debt.

The history of the West, especially since the Enlightenment, may be thematized in a variety of ways. Certainly, a central and often-noted theme in that history is the idea of freedom. History is indeed an uplifting story of increasing freedom but, as we will see, it is a history with a dark side as well, ending in indifference. Whenever the search for freedom degenerates into individualism, we have what Philip Rieff has labeled "the triumph of the therapeutic." With that dubious triumph, the idea of freedom becomes an ideology of the morally indifferent.

The idea of freedom is given definition by narrating what or whom persons conceive they need freedom *from.* For our purposes, five roughly chronological moments in that narration seem especially important.

Freedom from the State

The first moment in a history of freedom involves freedom from the arbitrary rule of the state. Beginning with the Magna Carta, furthered by the English and French revolutions, and later epitomized by the American Declaration and War of Independence, the idea of freedom has helped to define many people's expectations and hopes. Through the framework of freedom, the divine right of kings and hierarchies is exchanged for the sovereignty of the people themselves, precisely the "we the people" that begins the Constitution. The state can establish laws, levy taxes, and raise armies to protect the peace, but it can do so only with the consent of the governed. No taxation without representation, power to the people, workers of the world unite—the idea of freedom demands participation in self-government and self-determination, by and for the people. The obligations demanded by the state must be voluntarily and freely accepted; they cannot be imposed from without, but must emerge from the consent of the citizenry.

The idea of freedom overwhelms any opposition; it is a basic archetypal idea against which all arguments are futile. Even in countries where freedom is restricted, the restrictions are themselves seen as temporary and a voluntary act of the people in order to secure economic stability or to defend against an external threat. The history of political freedom in the West establishes the principle that the imposition of external authority or obligation is illegitimate. Collectively we cannot be made to do what we don't want to do. Heirs to the idea and history of political freedom, we are predisposed to reject any obligation, including moral obligations, that we do not voluntarily assume. Schooled in the notion of freedom, we regard moral imperatives as a voluntary "optional" responsibility. Imperatives must be freely accepted and in conformity to our desires; freedom is denied whenever we merely acquiesce to an externally imposed authority.

Freedom from Religion and the Church

The second moment in the history of freedom is similar to the first, only in this second instance people sought freedom from the authority of the church and a transcendent, unmoving God. Having secured freedom from the arbitrary rule of kings, people shifted their attention to securing freedom from the equally arbitrary demands of the church, whether those demands were experienced directly through a theocracy or indirectly in the form of cultural norms and expectations. Freedom from religion began with the Reformation and the splintering of a monolithic church and ended with the establishment of religious toleration and the process of secularization.

Toleration.   Initially, freedom from religion was dictated by a desire to escape the sectarian disputes of the sixteenth and seventeenth centuries. Toleration was needed because the strength of commerce was being exhausted by the interminable disputes about which of the competing religions was ultimately "true." In the face of a series of bloody civil and national wars, the establishment of the true religion became less an immediate concern than the establishment of civil tranquility. To the French politicians, the establishment of civil tranquility could be accomplished only by abandoning the search for a single public truth and by extending the right of individuals to believe what they would, as long as it did not directly harm others. As George Will succinctly stated it, toleration during this period was a blessing because it bred indifference. Indifference was a key to living peaceably with persons holding different beliefs and convictions than one's own.

John Locke's "Letter on Toleration," published in 1689, articulated an eventually triumphant movement to depoliticize, by privatizing, religious belief. Henceforth, and in contrast to what many would consider the inherent political nature of both Christianity and Judaism, religious and moral beliefs were a matter of private opinion rather than state policy. Belief was not amenable to state control, nor could the church deprive a people of their civil rights. I may believe that abortion or the salaries of corporate presidents are obscene in a nation where children go to bed hungry, but I do not have a right to impose directly those private beliefs on others; nor does the state have a right to impose the beliefs of others on me. There is, as Jefferson defined it, a separation of church and state. Public political questions are separable from private religious questions. Although the boundary between church and state, between public policy and private or religious "opinion," is always shifting (Is smoking, for example, a private choice or a matter of public health? Is prostitution a matter between consenting adults or violence against women?), the principle of religious toleration established in the seventeenth century both permitted persons of different faiths to live together and, not incidentally, effected a freedom from the religiously rooted demands of others. I may believe that persons should contribute to relief efforts in India but, because of the principle of toleration, neither I nor the state can impose civil penalties on someone who does not contribute.

The principle of religious toleration was institutionalized in the notion of the modern liberal state. Within the liberal conception of the state, the Aristotelian notion that ethics is a branch of politics is exchanged for a much narrower notion that politics is an arena in which the clash of self-interested individuals and groups is negotiated. Societal consensus on what constitutes the good life or on what kind of people we want to become is neither desirable nor necessary. On the one hand, it is not desirable because, as we have just seen, a liberal state must be tolerant of different beliefs and opinions in order to maintain civil tranquility. Consensus is not necessary, on the other hand, because, like a free market, it is assumed that a free competition between self-interested groups is perfectly self-balancing or correcting. Through the device of the invisible "benevolent hand" that Adam Smith first employed in explaining free economies, the political pursuit of private self-interest is transformed into the public good. We have a right, indeed a public duty, to pursue our own self-interest because, when all the self-interested groups are brought together, they balance one another in a way that creates the best society overall. Abandoning the search for public agreement on what constitutes a just or good society, the liberal state exchanges consensus for compromise and procedural safeguards. We work to implement our private beliefs, just as others work to implement theirs, on the expectation that the truth of the matter will be established in the long run.

The notion that religious questions and morals are private (saying that an issue is "religious" is a technique for confining it to the private realm) eliminates all but a few moral questions from public discussion or concern. The only moral issues on which public consensus is required involve issues establishing either the players or the rules by which the contest of ideas is to be conducted. Thus, issues such as equality, equal access to information and resources, and the informed consent of medical patients and consenting adults are important because they help to maintain and to protect the ability of autonomous moral agents to participate equally in the political power struggle. If one considers the issues associated with AIDS, for example, it is seemingly illegitimate to question the moral issue of homosexuality or drug abuse because we must be tolerant of alternative (not deviant) life-styles. It is legitimate, however, to raise the issue of an AIDS carrier's duty to inform his or her sexual partner about the potential risk of infection because that partner has a right to know so that he or she can make his or her own decision about the potential risks. The failure to be honest compromises or restricts the partner's ability to make a "free" decision and is thus subject to public censure.

Within the twin notions of toleration and the liberal state, indifference is thus a condition of civil tranquility. Our moral commitment, as a consequence, is limited to procedural norms and safeguards necessary for a fair contest between the combatants of the political power struggle. Outside that limited number of public concerns, moral issues are consigned to the realm of private opinion. Because private opinion carries little public force, the moral imperatives they substantiate can be ignored with impunity whenever they become inconvenient. Because the state must be tolerant, we are free to be indifferent.

Secularization. The freedom from religion established by the concept of religious toleration was reinforced subsequently by the process of secularization. Secularization is one way in which society liberates itself from religion. The moral imperatives of religion can be undermined if religion itself can be made to seem less sacred or authoritative. If the words of Moses and Jesus can be attributed to other people, to other places and times than their own, then the authority of those words becomes suspect and tenuous. If the miracles of scripture—the miracle of creation, the exodus, the resurrection—can be either explained or discounted through science, then the transcendent nature of religious authority is undermined. If the eternal doctrines of the church are the result of historical argument and development, then the eternal "truth" those doctrines proclaim seems less certain, more and more a product of human, fallible invention rather than of divine revelation.

Thus the techniques of the academics, employed to discern the truth, become in the hands of the inconvenienced a rationale for moral indifference. Tutored in a history of toleration and convinced that religious ideas are private or, worse yet, a matter of mere opinion, we are uncertain about where or when we can legitimately be intolerant. If my neighbors neglect their children in the pursuit of their careers, are sexually promiscuous, or are fanatic Redskins fans, can I legitimately be intolerant? At what point do I have the right to publicly condemn their actions, either directly or indirectly? At what point do my neighbors, in turn, have a right to condemn my indifference and self-indulgence? At what point can we be intolerant of indifference? As recently as in eighteenth-century France, the word *tolerance* was a pejorative term meaning a lax complacency toward evil. The reversal of that pejorative connotation in our own day displays the distance we have traversed on the road of freedom from religiously inspired morals.

Freedom from Reason
and Nature

Freedom from the state and religion was followed, in the eighteenth and nineteenth centuries, by a desire to be free from the obligations and constraints imposed by reason and nature. Although morals could no longer be grounded in particular, historical religions, Enlightenment thinkers believed that a universal moral order and coherence were nevertheless discernible in reason or nature. Kant's categorical imperative attempted to establish morals on the basis of reason alone, whereas in the Romantic movement, nature was supposed to tutor us not only in serenity but also in goodness. Morally disinherited from an absolute transcendent God, believers in the immanent God could nevertheless discern right and wrong in their own world, in reason and nature. Beneath apparent diversity, persons searched in the expectation that a perennial, universal religion and ethic would be discovered. Moral allegiances once sworn to the church found ready and compelling substitutes in a host of immanent or this-worldly faiths, in the inevitable progress of science, evolution, or the perennial philosophy articulated by the likes of Aldous Huxley.

Ironically, especially when viewed retrospectively, the substitution of an immanent for a transcendent God, of concern with this world rather than the next world, initially created a tremendous impetus for moral commitment. If God could not save us directly, through transcendent omnipotence, then it was our responsibility to save ourselves. Faith in the ability of humankind to improve the world is reasonable when viewed against a backdrop of increasing wealth, prosperity, and power. People in the late nineteenth century could point to improvements in science, health care, and transportation, to the abolition of slavery, to the incremental suffrage of women, and to a long period of peace as evidence that humankind was evolving to a higher state. Inconvenience on behalf of others is self-validating if my actions are seen to be a genuine help, that is, a genuine improvement in the world. Evidence of tangible progress, then as now, is a tremendous motivator for moral commitment.

The secularized, liberal faiths in science and social movements that emerged with prominence during the optimism of the nineteenth century were short-lived. By the beginning of World War I, substitute faiths had succumbed to the onslaught of pluralism, the new naturalism, and trench warfare. Ultimately, freedom from nature and reason became freedom from the future as well.

Freedom from the Future

In the twentieth century, the supposed universality and reality of reason and nature, upon which many of the substitute faiths rested, became more and more suspect. The study of history and cross-cultural or comparative studies in religion, sociology, and anthropology brought home and expressed an emerging cultural pluralism. If it can be shown that monogamy is not universal or inherent in nature but varies from culture to culture, then the moral imperative to remain faithful to one's spouse is undermined. If monogamy becomes inconvenient, then I can justify a lack of faithfulness by referring to the practices of Eskimos or Mormons. Pluralism weakens the hold of any single perspective and provides an excuse, when one is needed, to free oneself from the confines of one's own cultural dictates. The lesson of pluralism is that there are no invariant, universal standards to which one is obligated. Pluralism demonstrates that there are no self-evident truths, no inalienable rights, no indisputable human nature. We are free to pick and choose as we please. If morals are dependent on contexts, then there are fewer and fewer warrants for inconveniencing oneself on behalf of others. In the face of pluralism, commitment to a single set of moral imperatives may be dismissed as simply provincial.

The relativizing effects of cultural pluralism were reinforced by the emergence of modern naturalism. Increasingly, the criteria of the scientific laboratory became components in a pervasive worldview. Science defined what was real and what counted as evidence in ways that were not supportive of traditional ethics. Filtered through the lens of an insistent empiricism, nature no longer contained any inherent purpose, coherence, or meaning. The blind cosmos of the insistent empiricists simply *is;* there is no ultimate meaning or purpose, no explanation of *why*—only descriptions of mechanical, finite causes or random chance. No way exists for getting from *is* to *ought;* no distinction can be made between better or worse, higher or lower. As my former teacher Gabriel Vahanian once remarked, What does St. Augustine's prayer, "My heart is restless until it finds its rest in thee," mean when my heart is mechanical or is a transplanted organ from an accident victim?

The undermining of first religious, then natural and rational truths, helped eliminate the possibility of normative ethics. Traditionally, ethical discourse and judgment were either teleological or deontological. Persons ought to do such and such because, in so doing, they will fulfill either their inherent nature (*telos*) or the commandments of God, reason, nature, or some other ultimate authority. Within this traditional framework, ethical notions are inherently "factual"; to say that someone ought to do something is to say what course of action will "as a matter of fact" lead to humanity's end or to the fulfillment of the law. Moral situations are true or false in the same way that other statements are; action *x* either does or does not contribute to the fulfillment of humanity's end, reason, or God's commandments. Moral disputes about what we ought to do, at least in theory, are not interminable, for there are objective standards or ends against which moral disputes can be adjudicated.

The normative status of ethics becomes unclear whenever the "factual" nature on which it is based is eroded. If I can be persuaded that there is no inherent *telos,* no human nature, no universal reason, no commandments from God; if there is in nature no better or worse, higher or lower; if everything is relative—then the status of moral judgments becomes unclear. Shorn of their traditional framework,

ethical discourses and imperatives become suspect, less plainly legitimate, with the result that fewer and fewer situations are perceived
and defined in terms of their moral valence. Indeed, the term *moral*
itself becomes nonsensical and difficult to define. Increasingly, as the
criteria of the scientific laboratory become an accepted worldview,
moral statements appear to be wholly arbitrary. One moral imperative
seems no truer than any other; as a result, moral imperatives in
general contain no force. Ethics is nothing but an expression of private
desires or emotions. Friedrich Nietzsche articulated both the ontological death of God and the end of normative ethics. For him, as
for his successors, ethics is replaced by moral nihilism; what appears
as ethics is merely the expression of an ultimately self-serving will
to power. There are no appeals; there are only frightening, largely
unsubstantiated choices. Once a sign of liberation, the death of norms
means that we are, in the words of Jean-Paul Sartre, "condemned to
be free."

The undermining of ethics identified with the experience of
pluralism and the dominance of science in the nineteenth century
became widespread in Western culture with World War I. Faith in
progress or evolution, in the idealism of reason and nature, came to
an abrupt end with the Great War. In the face of trench warfare
(and later the Holocaust, nuclear weapons, and pollution), confidence
in the perfectibility of humanity, in our ability to save ourselves,
seemed less and less cogent. For those predisposed to religious belief,
a period of disillusionment created a return to neo-orthodoxy and
trust in divine intervention; for those less disposed to religion, however, disillusionment with progress became a rationale for doing
nothing. As long as the future can be made better, the obligation to
contribute to that future is strong. If, however, the future holds neither
promise nor hope, if destiny is replaced merely by one day after
another, we are then free from the moral burden and imperatives of
history. Discouragement and cynicism are an apologetic for freeing
oneself from the obligations of the future. If there is no future, or if
the future contains little possibility for improvement, then there is
no obligation to work toward it. Inconvenienced, I can dismiss the
constraints of the future by saying, "What does it matter anyway?"

Freedom from Others

The absolute freedom of existentialism, negatively articulated by
Nietzsche as nihilism, finds a cultural symbol in the figure of Freud.
Freedom from nature and reason becomes, with Freud, freedom from

community. Regardless of his original intention, Freud has come to represent the fifth and final moment to our story—freedom from the obligations and constraints inherent in living with others. The ultimate freedom is the freedom of a strident autonomous individual, the rugged individualism celebrated in the writings of Thoreau and the American myths of the entrepreneur and the cowboy, who neither owes nor expects any form of societal commitment. Philip Rieff describes Freudianism as the "triumph of the therapeutic" because the emergence of the psychological "virtuoso" signals the disintegration of a traditional culture of restraint and obligation to others.

Freud maintained that living in society always requires the sacrifice of individuality. Neurosis occurs because our instinctual drives are repressed by the cultural norms and expectations we internalize as the superego. Civilization requires cooperation, a cooperation that means, inevitably, the renunciation or subordination of private desire. Within a therapeutic culture, one must always do what one wants to do; anything else is a loss of independence and individuality. The contemporary idiom of self-realization, of doing one's own thing, of living in the here and now, spontaneous and free, is a popularized version of Freud's presumptions about individuals and society in *Civilizations and Its Discontents.* For Freud, freedom and the well-being of the individual rest on an ability to resist the moral imperatives of others. Rather than finding completion, satisfaction, and fulfillment in community (as maintained by traditional conceptions of culture), the individual envisioned by Freud finds happiness in escaping the restrictions and common ideals endemic to living with others. Firmly fixed on the goal of self-expression, the ideal of community must be overcome. Concern for society, for others, is exchanged for concern with oneself, one's own identity and quest.

Moral guilt is a wasted emotion, as Rieff says, a "pathology of moral aspiration." Guilt is illegitimate because society does not have a right to impose moral oughts on individuals. Moral commitment is a problem precisely because it signals the constraints and obligations of living with other people; freedom is an unassailable right to growth and self-expression. My commitment to my spouse, my children, my community restricts my freedom, imposes limits to what I can do and where I can go, on what I can spend my time and money. Whenever these limits become too constricting, I have a right to, as Tom Sawyer said, "light out for the territories." My guilt, that nagging sense that I should contribute to hunger relief or work for peace, is successfully anesthetized whenever I am persuaded that such activities illegitimately restrict my freedom. If traditional beliefs and ideals about moral commitments get in the way of my freedom, I can escape their pull and undermine their authority by saying that they are cultural illusions, class ideologies, or middle-class hang-ups. Therapy, as a debunking form of analysis, is a strategy of unbelief and detachment from the ethical frameworks (myths of commitment) that cement a moral community. The psychological virtuoso congratulates herself or himself for being honest and brave enough to face reality as it is without illusion and, in the process, unwittingly supplies an apologia for indifference. Moral indifference is a goal precisely because it creates the greatest possible scope for individual desire and self-concern. I am, as an autonomous individual, most free precisely when I am most indifferent to the needs of others. Freedom is not only a political, religious, and intellectual necessity; it is a psychological necessity as well. Indifference is a condition of ultimate freedom.

Free to Be Indifferent

The familiar history of freedom narrates a series of lessons in moral indifference. Stated summarily, these lessons (which used to be called *morals*) include the following propositions: (1) Moral imperatives are voluntary; they cannot be legitimately imposed upon us by the state or by institutional religion. (2) Moral impulses are largely private in origin. Toleration in the service of civil tranquility requires a studied indifference to all but a select number of moral issues involving either procedural safeguards or the maintenance of autonomous moral agents. (3) Analogous to a free economy, a free moral economy permits the unrestrained pursuit of self-interest; through the device of the invisible hand of the political process, private vice is transformed into civic virtue. (4) The moral dictates inherent in reason, nature, and religion are illusory. Ethics has no ontological grounding and is dependent on the emotion and the will of individuals or groups. (5) Personal fulfillment requires freedom from the restraints of cultural norms and expectations. Freedom is a psychological, as well as a political, religious, and intellectual necessity.

So stated, the ideas of indifference endemic to the history of freedom are a ready defense against the inconveniences of moral commitment, a rudimentary apologetic for moral inertia and sloth. Inconvenienced by a pesky neighbor, by the moral demands of my spouse or friends to support gay rights or the "freedom fighters" in Nicaragua, I can retreat into an undisturbed lethargy, secure in the knowledge that I live in a society that tolerates and protects my indifference. The church may criticize my stance towards birth control, sexual behavior, or abortion, but no matter. I can successfully undermine the authority of my more moralistic opponents by rehearsing the very human foibles of the church and its agents. Whenever my desires exceed the constraints of what may seem reasonable or natural, I can dismiss any lingering sense of guilt or violation with the idea that, finally, moral imperatives are nothing but a matter of opinion. Equipped with the ideas of Freud, obligations I may have toward others are secondary to my own right to unrestrained growth and self-expression.

On one level, the history of freedom provides a series of excuses for moral indifference. More subtly, it also constitutes an implicit "mythic" framework through which we unself-consciously see or interpret experience. If I unquestioningly accept the notion that personal fulfillment takes priority over the imperative to help others, then the decision whether I should give to famine relief or buy a new car does not arise. If, for me, the world is simply an amoral arena, then the quest for marital fidelity, for honesty in business, or for a greater equality in the distribution of wealth has no foundation. The notion that I, as a citizen of a tolerant liberal state, have a right to tell (much less constrain) my neighbors to spend more time with their children is simply not, in William James's words, a "live option." My "right" (freedom) to go trekking in Nepal, my decision to buy products on the basis of price rather than on the social responsibility of the company involved—such questions never come to mind because the myth of the idea of freedom insulates me from any possible alternative action. Persuaded and beguiled by an invisible rhetoric of indifference, I do not examine the morality of my actions and the application of moral categories remains uncertain. Moral sloth, as a result, is less a deliberate, self-conscious decision than an unwitting acceptance of a cultural birthright. Acknowledgment of my obligation to others is the largely invisible casualty of a history of freedom.

Moral challenges vary as contexts vary. The idea of freedom successfully challenged and undermined the moral authority of kings, the church, nature, reason, and finally community. Confronting the various sources of moral authority was perhaps the most challenging moral question facing previous generations. For our generation, however, the idea of freedom, whenever it degenerates into moral indifference, is itself a major stumbling block to a morally committed future. Freedom, as an apologetic for indifference, is at the center of the moral dilemma most characteristic of our time. Overcoming indifference requires, ironically, overcoming a history of freedom.

CHAPTER SIX

From Indifference
to Commitment

Myths and ideologies functioning as myths are central ingre-
dients to moral indifference. By helping to define what is real and
important, they either encourage or impede how well we see and
acknowledge moral imperatives. Consequently, they directly influence
how we respond to and embody our moral commitments. Myths and
ideologies are thus present in each of the three dimensions we have
defined in chapter 1 as being essential to moral commitment: seeing,
acknowledging, and acting. Debunking the myths of indifference is
a necessary prelude to moral commitment. It is for this reason that
we have presented illustrative myths of indifference from popular
religion, culture, and political ideology in chapters 3, 4, and 5.

Although pervasive, myths of indifference are not the only
impediment to moral commitment. Nor, for that matter, does the
framework of seeing, acknowledging, and acting exhaust the requisites
for moral commitment. To understand how moral commitment fails,
we must understand more fully how it succeeds. A constructive theory
of how commitment succeeds provides a clue to those elements that,
if absent, contribute to moral indifference.

Moral commitment represents the integration of three elements:
experience, a committing framework of interpretation, and power/
embodiment. These three categories provide a basis for the categories
of seeing, acknowledging, and acting we introduced earlier. As we
will see shortly, experience provides a basis for seeing, just as moral
frameworks of interpretation provide a basis for acknowledging our
moral obligations. And finally, the notion of power/embodiment, as

both a basis for action in its own right and the *telos* of experience and moral frameworks of interpretation, completes the inventory of what needs to be present before moral commitment is fulfilled.

Confronted with a recalcitrant indifference, we search for absences, for what is not there. Indifference is symptomatic that something is missing. The identification of that missing element—whether experience, a moral framework of interpretation, or power/embodiment—is a crucial and necessary first step toward moral commitment.

Experience

Experience comes in two primary forms, real and imaginary, and both forms are important to moral commitment. Real experience is important because it challenges and expands the status quo of our prior experience in a way that is difficult to deny, whereas imaginative experience is important because it provides a means for both vicarious experience and a transcendence of what is.

Real Experience.   A situation elicits experience to the extent that it "signifies an active and alert commerce" with the world. The phrasing is John Dewey's, and it was he who used the term *aesthetic* honorifically to designate a genuine experience. Experience represents literally coming to one's senses. Experience occurs whenever we are challenged to see new things or, alternatively, to see old things in a new way; it combines precepts with concepts, what is with our interpretation of what is. Experience is an encounter with something real, something beyond our fantasies and solipsistic illusions. We unself-consciously describe our encounters with dramatic and significant situations as "that was really an experience."

Moral reflection begins with a confrontation with a real situation, with what is. Dewey suggested that aesthetic, that is genuine, experience is specifically a moral imperative to the extent that it is able to challenge prejudice and established custom by exposing us to the real. Experience is a bumping against something not ourselves. A prejudice that people on welfare are lazy or stupid can be disrupted if it can be shown that most people on welfare are incapable of working because of a disability or because of their responsibility to small children. The unself-conscious assumption that we live in a righteous nation can be transformed if it can be shown that our government has participated in illegal and covert operations to overthrow the government of another nation. The personal experience of prolonged unemployment can test an unexamined faith in economic justice. In instances such as these, the experience of what is probes the limits of our thought and prior experience. Experience undermines complacency and the indifference of established states of thought and feeling.

Experience, a genuine encounter with what is really the case, is an essential element of ethics. Conversely, the absence of experience contributes to indifference. Experience is the *is*, apart from which there cannot be a discrepancy between *is* and *ought*. Nevertheless, experience is often threatening, sometimes unpleasant, and almost always subversive to the status quo. The avoidance of experience, and the indifference that follows in the wake of that avoidance, routinely occurs on both physical and ideological levels.

On the physical level, we frequently insulate ourselves from exposure to potentially unpleasant situations. Suburbanites insulate themselves from the poverty and dishevelment of urban slums. One may read about the disease and malnutrition in Africa, but it is relatively easy to ignore its moral call when surrounded by the sounds of lawns being watered and the smells of backyard cookouts. The problems of the aged or the homeless contain no moral obligation if everyone I associate with is young, prosperous, and healthy. We willingly and unquestioningly live within institutions that allow us to avoid people who are sick, dying, and less advantaged. Ethical problems are seldom pleasant; as a result, we have a natural tendency to avoid or isolate ourselves from the situations whose moral imperatives would challenge our complacency.

The denial or avoidance of experience occurs on an ideological as well as a physical level. It is exceedingly easy to insulate oneself by ignoring or summarily dismissing opinions that differ from one's own. Indeed, the term *indifference* may at times be little more than a way to categorically dismiss someone who holds different commitments than one's own. If the primary responsibility of Christianity is to save souls, social issues need not be seriously considered. If feeding the hungry and clothing the naked are the primary imperatives behind the gospel, then evangelical efforts to save souls can be dismissed as quaint vestiges of the past and thus socially irresponsible. If national defense is the first responsibility of government, then the importance of food stamps and reindustrialization is literally secondary; if people get what they deserve, then the problem of economic injustice is illusionary. On the physical level, we say that people who deliberately or unself-consciously avoid experience are sheltered or inexperienced; on the ideological level, we say that such persons are closed-minded and inflexible. If ethics begins with an encounter with what is, then the avoidance of experience, whether deliberate or circumstantial, is a common and well-worn path to indifference.

Imagination.   Experience occurs whenever we are exposed to new situations or ways of seeing, whenever we become aware, or whenever we are unable to maintain our prejudices in the face of recalcitrant facts. Typically, such experiences occur in real life, either in direct personal experience or by observing the experience of others. Significantly, however, they can also occur because of an encounter with imaginative works of literature or art. Passages and images gleaned from a novel can be as memorable and can have as much impact on our lives as real-life experience. *Uncle Tom's Cabin,* for example, confronted people with the question of slavery in a way that was more effective and compelling than the actual existence of slavery. An imaginative portrayal of a nuclear accident can be more terrifying and immediate than the real-life threats of a local nuclear installation. Imaginative renderings of an actual event or an entirely fictionalized account can present us with situations no less shattering to our prejudices and limited experience than real life.

The advantages of imaginative situations are two. First, by imagining what a situation would be like, we are able vicariously to experience a situation in a nonthreatening way. I may not have the courage to live in a ghetto or to flee from El Salvador, but I can do so vicariously through imaginative accounts. I may not be willing to help others, but I may nevertheless experience the rewards of philanthropy by reading about someone else's experience. We often do what we first do in our imaginations; we often see what we first have seen through imaginative literature. Through imaginative accounts of real or fictional events, we become inspired.

With the nuclear issue, the imagination has a particularly important function. Through the forethought afforded by the imagination, we can experience the total destruction of nuclear war in a way that may prevent it from occurring. By mentally seeing the dead and injured, the destroyed cities and towns, the burned and sick, we can create an imaginative context for preventing nuclear war. Most often, ethics responds to real situations and events but, with the nuclear issue, imagination must precede experience because the actual experience itself would be terminal. A similar use of the imagination is required in irreversible ecological issues. Once a species or the ozone layer is gone, it is gone forever. Any issue dealing with irreversible consequences establishes an especially telling link between imagination and moral reflection.

In addition to providing a means of forethought and vicarious experience, imagination provides the capacity to envision the possibility of or to engender the hope of a different way of life. Imagination is the foundation for the *ought* apart from which ethics is impossible. Ethics begins with a discrepancy between the *is* and an imagined *ought*. Without the rudimentary ability to imagine something beyond what is, without, for example, an imagined state of economic or social justice, the civil rights struggle and liberation movements would be stillborn. Dreams and visions of the way it could and ought to be precede reality and make a new reality possible. Without hope, without imagining how things could be, indifference either of despair or complacency is inevitable.

A defining characteristic of imaginary situations is their ability to compel attention. For whatever reason, we notice them. The imaginative rendering of real events by a journalist or historian expresses more than just a list of one thing after another. Sitting listlessly in front of the television set, we suddenly become alert and interested. We notice, and thus expose ourselves to experience. With imagination, we do not simply have the facts; we have the facts presented in a compelling way, re-creation rather than mere entertainment. We speak of art capturing our attention in a way that makes us forgetful of ourselves and our self-interest. We get lost or caught up in a story in a way that permits us to transcend our own egocentric concerns. Through the skill of the imaginative artist, including the artistry of the journalist, our sympathies may be awakened and drawn to persons who, in real life, we would dismiss or ignore altogether. It is for this reason that Keats accurately referred to poets as the "unacknowledged legislators" of the world.

The ability of art to compel attention is especially important in confronting the indifference of the middle class. The principle problem of the middle class is the lack of any recalcitrant problems Ironically, affluence leads to moral deprivation. What can liberation mean to those who have already achieved economic and social freedom? What can the problems of an inadequate health care system mean to those who have insurance and access to the best medicine money can buy? The middle class does not have a need to change; indeed, quite the contrary. More often, it needs to defend the status quo of its privileged position. Confronted with the growing specter of homelessness, the middle class is indifferent or threatened and defensive. In contrast, if an artist successfully compels attention to the story of the homeless as, for example, Jonathan Kozol's account of *Rachel and Her Children,* then the discrepancy between the *is* of the disenfranchised and the *is* of the middle class becomes a compelling if unspoken entrance to the way things ought to be. We may be repelled by the odor and dirt of the homeless who adorn Grand Central Station, but their stories, imaginatively rendered, can undermine our complacency.

Imagination is linked with forethought and vicarious experience, with the transcendence of the what is to a vision of what could or ought to be.

The Domestication of Experience and Imagination.   Experience, whether real or imaginal, represents a form of transcendence of prior experience and the facticity of day-to-day reality. Indifference is undermined by any kind of transcendence. But experience alone does not ensure moral commitment. Experience is potentially morally activating; it potentially subverts moral indifference. But with that potential, there is also danger. Rubem Alves pointed out the dangers of what he described as "the domesticated imagination" in reference to imaginary works of literature. His observations apply equally to actual experience. The undermining of indifference by experience requires being cautious about the ways experience itself can contribute to moral indifference.

Imagination fails to be morally activating—indeed, encourages indifference—whenever it is alienated. An alienated imagination, according to Alves, is characteristically escapist and solipsistic. Instead of using the imagination as a means for transcending and thus transforming the given, an alienated imagination acquires an autonomy of its own and becomes a substitute world. Instead of pointing to the real world, it becomes its own world. Diverted and entertained by this secondary world of "bread and circuses," we may leave undisturbed the real world in need of transformation. I was going to help my neighbor, but the game between the Celtics and the Lakers was on television. The needs of the hungry or the intricacies of a flawed health care system remain unchallenged as long as we are lost in the entertainment of sports and movies or, alternatively, as long as we are engaged in the experiences afforded by rafting trips and Himalayan treks. Alves concludes that ethical thought comes to an abrupt end whenever imagination or experience "exhausts itself in itself. It becomes a sort of spiritual masturbation: The pleasure which consciousness finds in imagination does not fertilize the world." The pleasures of an alienated imagination divert us into the impotence of moral indifference.

Experiences, both real and imaginal, are double-edged. They may take us toward moral imperatives, but they may also provide a means of escaping those same imperatives. Whether an experience elicits a response of commitment or one of escape is partially determined by what we bring to it, by how we interpret it. Experience is only potentially a moral situation. It is never self-interpreting, although it may seem as such. Confronted by a lunch counter sit-in during the early sixties, the segregationist sees blacks and northern troublemakers breaking the law and stirring things up, whereas the integrationist sees a further confirmation of southern racism and injustice. Neither the segregationist nor the integrationist is likely to say that what he or she sees is an interpretation; on the contrary, what is seen is just "the way things are." Nevertheless, on reflection, the mediation of an interpretative step between what is and what is perceived is apparent. In addition to experience, moral situations require an interpretation. Marjorie Green reminds us of the importance of interpretation to ethics with the simple, arresting sentence, "Only by an act of evaluation [we would say interpretation], do we call the story of Auschwitz mass murder and so assimilate it to human history rather than to chemistry or population genetics."

Moral Frameworks
of Interpretation

Experience, a confrontation with both what is and what ought to be, provides a basis for moral seeing. Experience alone, however, is only the first ingredient to moral commitment. In addition to experience, moral commitment also requires interpretation. No experience is morally self-interpreting, as Marjorie Green suggests. Apart from an act of interpretation, experience is only a potential moral situation, in two senses. First, interpretation represents the way or the framework through which we see an experience; it is the reference point—the presuppositions, the stories, and the past experiences—through which we make sense of the experiences we confront. And second, moral frameworks of interpretation are the means by which we are connected to moral imperatives. Through moral frameworks of interpretation, we acknowledge, and thus become responsible for, our moral obligations.

Levels of Interpretation.   Think for a moment of an elderly hospital patient, lying comatose and supported by a life-support system. The patient's experience of the hospital, the staff, the diagnosis, and the daily struggle to stay alive implies a host of interpretative questions.

The first and perhaps most fundamental question is this: Does the experience of the dying patient constitute a problem? Is there a discrepancy between what is and what ought to be, that is both perceptible and amenable to mitigation? (Problems that are not mitigable are tragedies.) Defining an experience as problematic requires seeing not only the *is* of a situation but an *ought* as well. Categorizing the patient as "sick" suggests an envisioned context of wellness, whereas categorizing the patient as "elderly" may suggest an appropriate process of dying. Always in the background is a vision of the desirable, imagined state against which the actual state is being compared.

A second question quickly follows the first: If the experience is problematic, then is the experience a specifically *moral* problem? There are many sorts of problems, not all of which belong to the realm of morality. For the physician, the immediate problem may be keeping the patient alive; for the family, the problem may be a daily increasing debt; for the hospital, the problem may be maintaining a high bed-occupancy rate. The patient in each of these instances is the focal point of a problem; however, how the problem is defined varies from the context or framework of interpretation within which the patient is seen. The problem changes according to the interpretation and, often, according to the self-interest of the interpreter.

While acknowledging the problems indigenous to the respective positions of the physician, hospital administrator, and family, the moralist sees the situation of the dying patient as a specifically moral problem, through a specifically moral framework. A moral framework of interpretation enables the ethicist to ask specifically moral questions, rather than questions of economics or biology or occupancy-rate demographics. Questions of economics and biology may help in answering moral questions but they are not, in themselves, moral questions.

What is a specifically moral problem? Provisionally, we may say that a moral problem speaks or responds to a discrepancy between how we actually live and our vision of how we ought to live. The moralist is finally concerned with the good life and how it can best be achieved. Given the experience of our patient, the physician confronts a biological, medical problem: "How do I keep the patient alive?" The family and hospital face an economic problem: "Who is to pay for the care?" The ethicist, however, confronts a larger or more encompassing question: "Should people die in this way? Is this the way we ought to live and die?" Answering these moral questions establishes the parameters within which to frame the biological and economic questions. Ought the physician keep the patient alive through extraordinary means? Ought the patient or the patient's family alone be responsible for the medical costs, or should those costs be shared by the community at large? Ought the primary financial beneficiary of a patient's illness be the individual physician, the researchers who benefit through grants to eradicate disease, or the insurance companies? Sooner or later, the actions of the physician and hospital administrator find their context in the moral problem of how we ought to live. Although the biological question rests with the physician and the cost question rests with the hospital administrator, the moral question belongs to all of us as we collectively muddle through to a vision of how we are to live together. Each of us is an ethicist in a way that each of us is not a physician or a bureaucrat.

Ought questions can typically be answered in at least two ways. The moral problem elicited by a dying patient can, for example, be seen as either a technical problem or a problem of moral vision. On the one hand, the problem may be one of access to the technology and resources of the medical profession. Granting the sacredness of life, persons have a right to the best of medical technology, regardless of the cost. At least in part, Medicare, health insurance, and health-maintenance organizations are responses to the moral problem—that is, injustice—associated with persons not having access to health care. People should have access to care, regardless of their ability to pay. When they don't a discrepancy emerges between what is and what ought to be. With "technical" moral problems, solutions are sought within a framework of accepted assumptions. As a result, the *ought* question is less of a concern than the question of how the *ought* can be achieved.

Alternatively, the moral problem of the elderly dying patient may be seen as a problem of moral vision. For many, the case of the elderly patient is an exemplary instance of the Faustian bargain our society has made with technology and medical science. In this second interpretation, expending vast sums of technological and financial resources on the indefinite extension of life is nonsense, especially when, for example, these same resources could be used to help the millions of American children who never see a dentist. The problem in this second interpretation is not a technical problem of access to medical care but a pursuit of medical technology that goes beyond the limits of a meaningful life, on the one hand, and the allocation of our society's resources on the other. The patient is not sick; he or she is merely old. As distinguished from a technical problem, a problem of moral vision asks what ought to be in a more fundamental way: Is it true that this patient should not be allowed to die? Should resources be expended in preserving this life? How should people die? Hospices are a response to this second interpretation of the problem, just as Medicare is a response to the first interpretation. Questions of moral vision are identified by their questioning of basic assumptions about how the world should be.

In the first interpretation, the patient exists in a relatively stable context. The moral problem, consequently, is reduced to a question of technique. Given our assumptions about health and the existing health care system, how can we increase access to health care? The alternative interpretation suggests a broader context. The sacredness of life at *any* cost suggested in the first interpretation is itself problematic. The problem is not only with the medical care system; the problem *is* the medical care system itself and what it presumes about health and well-being. Although both interpretations speak to the good life, to how we should live, the second does so at a more fundamental level; there are fewer presumptions about what constitutes the good life. The second interpretation acknowledges that ethics is inseparable from an imaginative envisioning of oughts.

The analysis of the elderly hospital patient may be extended to other moral dilemmas as well. Consider, for example, the "population problem." Is the problem one of too many people, or is it one of unequal distribution of resources? Is feminism a problem of access to positions of power within corporations, or is it a problem concerning how corporations should be restructured? Is national defense a problem about how we can afford to arm the free world, or is it a problem involving our conception of what constitutes the greatest threat to our national sovereignty? How one reacts to a potentially moral situation comes to light after a long line of interpretative acts—acts that, in most instances, are made unself-consciously and seemingly without choice. More often than not, a "decision" is merely a ritual enactment of the presumptions with which we began.

Frameworks of moral interpretation have a variety of sources. Traditionally, notions about the good life have come from religion, in symbols such as the kingdom of God. But such notions may also come from popular culture, political ideologies, and personal experiences. Even within the same source, different versions of a moral framework may emerge. For example, the notion of salvation carries a different connotation for the religious conservative and the religious liberal. The essential point is that moral vision requires a specifically moral framework of interpretation, regardless of its source. Moral indifference, almost by definition, occurs whenever there is an absence of moral frameworks of interpretation.

The transformation of experience into a specifically moral situation comes through a process of interpretation. Interpretation defines an experience as problematic, categorizes the problem as specifically moral in nature, and assesses the type of moral problem it is, whether a problem of technique or vision. Without interpretation, experience remains an invisible black hole of indifference. Normally, even for professional ethicists, only a small portion of experience goes through a deliberate, self-conscious process of interpretation. More often than not, interpretation and experience collapse into one another. We simply see a situation as "it is," with little recognition that what we see is dependent on an interpretation. The segregationist of the 1950s does not, from his or her perspective, deliberately "interpret" blacks at a lunch counter as troublemakers; the segregationist simply sees that they are troublemakers. Buying Nestlé chocolate is not a moral problem, unless that act is interpreted as relating to the detrimental effects of marketing baby formula in third-world countries. Indifference occurs wherever there is a collapse, an absence of distance, between experience and interpretation.

Myths of Commitment. Moral frameworks of interpretation, deployed in what we have described as levels of interpretation, are complemented by "committing frameworks of interpretation." Levels of interpretation describe how we see a moral situation, whereas committing frameworks establish a more direct connection between that situation and my response to it. Chapters 3, 4, and 5 examined examples of what we have called the myths of indifference that impede moral commitment. If, however, myths can impede moral commitment, then the opposite may also be true. That is to say, myths of indifference may find their opposite in corresponding "myths of commitment"—models that orient our understanding and behavior and that encourage rather than hinder moral commitment. Overcoming indifference requires not the abandonment of myth altogether but the exchange of one sort of myth for another.

The exodus story is an exemplary and familiar myth of commitment. The myth arose, of course, from the story of the Israelite people being delivered from bondage in Egypt. When reduced to a set of propositions, the story contains many possible meanings, that is, many possible interpretations. In contrast to the myths of dualism, individualism, and merited inequality examined earlier, however, the exodus story presents a universe that cannot be divided into body and spirit or individualized (proportioned) according to earned merit.

Liberation theology in particular has emphasized that the exodus story is about the liberation of a poor and subjugated people. Salvation for them was neither individual nor exclusively spiritual. The Israelites were saved in a political, this-worldly act of leaving Egypt. Salvation meant physically moving from one place to another. Furthermore, salvation meant the establishment of a nation, rather than the daring escape of a few individuals. The exodus myth encourages us to see that God cares about and acts in the events and history of this world, that God is concerned with our physical as well as spiritual well-being, and that salvation is a collective, rather than an individual, event.

Importantly, God's salvation came to the poor and subjugated in the exodus story. God's salvation was not reserved for the affluent, the intelligent, or even the morally virtuous. On the contrary, salvation came as a gift to the disinherited rather than as a reward for merit or achievement. As heirs to the tradition of the exodus, we are reminded that we too began as slaves and that our salvation, like theirs, is equally unmerited. Salvation comes from God and not from our own efforts. Because of the exodus story, we are reminded that we are no better or more virtuous than the poor; on the contrary, we may be under a special obligation to work toward their physical as well as spiritual salvation. Indeed, because salvation is a collective rather than an individual event, because the poor and the middle class are part of one nation, our salvation is indivisibly linked with that of the poor. The story of rising up from poverty has often been distorted into a success story ("We started as slaves, but look at us now"), but in its truest form, the exodus story informs our vision and encourages our will on behalf of the disenfranchised and enslaved.

The exodus story is an exemplary myth of commitment because it helps us both to see and to acknowledge moral imperatives. From the purview of the myth, we see that physical and spiritual well-being cannot be conveniently divided. We cannot save people's souls while conveniently forgetting their bodies. God cares about this world, and we should do likewise. Second, the myth encourages us to see that salvation is a corporate event. Salvation is not about individuals finding Jesus and being saved; it is about an entire people moving toward a promised land. By emphasizing the corporate character of salvation, we undermine the notion of individual merit and encourage an acknowledgment that the fates of both the poor and the middle class are inseparable. In this, as in so many other instances, acknowledgment follows in the wake of how I see the world. I *acknowledge* an obligation to the poor to the extent that I *see* that the poor and the middle class are members of one community and that my salvation is indivisibly linked with the salvation of others.

In addition to myths of indifference, there are myths that bewitch us into commitment. The exodus story is but one of many possible myths of commitment. In recent years, widely circulated works such as *Habits of the Heart* and *Statecraft as Soulcraft* have called for the revitalization of biblical and republican myths as means of renewing our mutual, civil commitments. The story that we are fulfilled and completed in community rather than as isolated individuals is a powerful myth of commitment that extends back to the *Republic* of Plato. If moral commitment requires, on the one hand, debunking myths of indifference, it also requires, on the other hand, a re-enchantment by those myths of commitment indigenous to our culture. Enchantment as well as disenchantment has its uses in a moral economy.

Power

Moral situations combine experience, whether real or imaginary, with moral frameworks of interpretation. Moral situations, in turn, are a necessary but insufficient ingredient to moral commitment. In addition to experience and moral frameworks of interpretation, moral commitment also requires an empowerment/embodiment of the moral life. Power/embodiment is the *telos* toward which experience and moral frameworks of interpretation are directed. Moral commitment is inseparable from questions of power or embodiment in at least three senses.

First, power (the ability to change things) is a precondition of moral action. Without the ability to effect change, a moral question as to whether to take one course of action rather than another has no grounding. Issues such as birth control, environmental pollution, and the sustaining of life through organ transplants arise precisely because areas that were once beyond human control are now firmly within our grasp. Before science achieved the ability to develop life in a test tube, the issue of *in vitro* fertilization was not a moral issue. The scope of ethics increases in proportion to the increasing power of the human community to change things, as more and more areas move from being natural to artificial. How power is extended and into which areas—whether research is conducted on new strains of barley and oats, on satellite communications or new weapons systems—affect the course and questions that ethics will eventually confront. Ethical issues emerge and follow in the wake of how and by whom and for what purposes power is extended.

The second way power and indifference are interrelated involves a failure to acknowledge that all embodiments are expressions of power. Power is necessarily embodied and vice versa. We are indifferent because we do not see the connections between tax policy and an increase in poverty, between the federal budget and the lives of individuals in our own communities. Too often we are insulated from the effects of bad public policy or corrupt officials; or, worse, we accept such officials and policies as an inevitable part of a recalcitrant bureaucracy. The strategy of civil disobedience rests, in part, on making the otherwise invisible effects of policies visible, that is, embodied for all to see. The infamous bridge at Selma, Alabama, displayed for all to see the policy and attitudes of a recalcitrant white racism. Television coverage of the Vietnam War brought home the embodied policy of the Johnson administration. Indifference occurs whenever the connections between power and moral commitments are absent.

Because power and embodiment are inseparable, moral reflection is a practical, pragmatic discipline whose goal is the application of power to particular situations and contexts to bring about a congruence between the *is* and the *ought*. If moral reflection is an art, it is a performing art like dance or music. Apart from the embodied dance, the dance does not exist; apart from the music, the score is incomplete. Analogously, moral concepts, ideas, and visions—apart from their embodiment—remain unfinished, a silent and motionless embodiment of indifference rather than commitment. The consequences of holding to one set of moral commitments rather than another is always played out in some form of embodiment. A moral impulse for the preservation of the environment is literally disembodied apart from the regulation of toxic waste and car emissions. Sympathy for the poor apart from action is either hypocrisy or sentimentalism. To paraphrase William James, moral commitments are real to the extent that they are real in their effects. The absence of those effects defines a practical form of indifference.

Ironically, when separated from embodiment, moral insight— a newly awakened sense and even moral outrage about abortion, for example—may actually contribute to moral indifference. It is immensely satisfying, indeed beguiling, to be knowledgeable about the causes of unemployment and the shrinking middle class. Simply knowing about or understanding a situation brings about a sense of being on top of things, an order and structure to experience that is, in itself, satisfying. The myth of education is that knowledge alone is sufficient. The academic ethicists, with neither audience nor stake in the outcome of a moral decision, remain indifferent. The gaunt images and squalor of refugee camps televised on the evening news, the racism and injustice depicted in a movie like *Cry Freedom,* become a form of entertainment and diversion rather than an impetus for action. Being aware, "grappling with complex moral issues," as a current phrase expresses it, seems better and somehow morally superior to not knowing. But apart from action, awareness alone remains an insidious trap of moral reflection. "The aware person," Richard Hoehn reminds us, "has a sense of moral OK-ness without doing much to alleviate suffering or bring about justice in a troubled world. The feeling of being one who knows may be satisfying, but it is not terribly helpful to those who suffer great injustice."

Power and embodiment are interrelated in a third and final sense. Often, well-meaning persons do not act because of a sense of individual powerlessness. In many instances such powerlessness is more perceived than actual. For such people who are burdened with a moral insight, the questions remain, What can I do? How can I help alleviate hunger or end the arms race or create a more equitable society? Oddly, the overwhelming feeling of powerlessness one feels in response to such questions is reassuring and provides an apologia for indifference: Because I am powerless, the burden and inconvenience of having to do something are lifted. As long as I am powerless, I have a ready excuse for failing to respond to a moral imperative.

The indifference of powerlessness may be overcome through the incremental acquisition of a sense of personal control and effectiveness. Personal effectiveness, the sense that I can do something, varies with the context. In many instances, moral effectiveness involves fairly routine knowledge and performances. If I see or encounter a disoriented drug addict on a city street, I may be dissuaded from providing assistance if I am uncertain about how I should act. Do I call a policeman or a local relief agency? Do I attempt to talk with the person directly? Do I act individually, or do I attempt to elicit the help of other passersby? I may want to help but, without basic knowledge and practice as to how to deal with such situations, I may lack the personal effectiveness to empower my best moral impulses. I look plaintively to see if anyone else is moving to help. Seeing no one, I walk past. Often persons fail to act because of a simple lack of practical knowledge about how to get from A to B.

The direct and immediate moral performance demanded on a city street has its counterpart in less direct moral responses. On an intermediate level, an acquaintance from seminary serves as an example. Assigned to a rural community in eastern Wyoming, he soon discovered the unavailability of local medical care. When farmers or ranchers were injured, he was powerless to help, except to rush them to a distant hospital. For my friend, the solution to such powerlessness, in the short term, involved learning emergency first aid and medicine. On the longer term, the solution lay in organizing local business-people to attract a physician to the community. The lack of medical care in rural communities is a moral as well as a medical problem. People should have access to emergency care, and they don't. Re-sponding to this problem morally requires gaining the power to act in an effective manner.

Direct, individual responses to moral situations are often criti-cized for being "Band-Aid" responses to systematic problems, and rightly so. Remembering the link between politics and ethics first suggested by Aristotle, we find that the most political and at the same time most indirect response to a moral situation may require acquiring the skills to change systems and institutions. I may do something immediately and directly about world hunger by writing a letter to my representative in Congress, but my effectiveness, my power to change things, will be greatly magnified if I learn how to work with others in the political process to introduce and gain support for the passage of legislation. In *Up from Apathy*, Hoehn recounts story after story of people who have gained a sense of personal effectiveness by getting policies implemented at their PTA, in county and state governments, and in Congress. "A few we-did-it experi-ences," he concludes, "a few victories . . . empower and sustain a person in the action world for a long period of time." Inaction, the concrete enactment of indifference, finds its opposite in the moral performances of people who know how and do get things done both through direct and indirect action. If a sense of personal effectiveness or power is absent, we lapse into the passive, childlike indifference of those who must wait and hope that others will affect moral change.

Moral Commitment
and Its Absence:
A Theory of Indifference

A theory of moral experience approaches moral indifference by way of absences. By suggesting why moral commitment succeeds, we hope to suggest why moral commitment fails as well.

Summarily, we have said that moral commitment represents the integration of three primary elements: experience (as a basis for seeing), moral frameworks of interpretation (as a basis for both seeing and acknowledging), and power/embodiment (as a basis for acting). If the absence of one of these elements contributes to indifference, then the diminution of indifference requires an appropriation of that which is absent, whether it be experience, interpretation, or power/embodiment. Exposure to the effects of moral problems, the reading of imaginative and idealistic literature, the nurturing and support of moral frameworks of interpretation, the undermining of what we have described as the myths of indifference, the acquisition of sufficient political skills to enact and embody our commitments—each of these steps may fill an absence, the black hole of moral indifference. Some people may confront indifference by creating situations, both real and imaginary, in which they can experience discrimination or homelessness or insider trading. Others may challenge indifference by discerning and undermining the effects of those myths that so shape our vision that we are indifferent by default. Still others may overcome moral sloth by demonstrating how individual citizens can help enact legislation to support hunger programs and political reform. A theory of absences proves its worth if it accurately defines the missing elements to moral commitment.

The theory of moral indifference we propose is not exhaustive. Indeed, as our chapter on Niebuhr and his successors suggests, other more psychological reasons also have explanatory force. Nevertheless, this theory is a useful framework for discerning important impediments to moral commitment. An illustrative application of our theory to the three types of moral commitment—the individual, the political, and the intermediate—occupies our attention in the following chapter. As we will see, the absent element contributing to moral indifference—whether experience, interpretation, or power/embodiment—varies according to the level or type of moral issue being considered. By examining each of these levels in turn, we will discover additional clues about how moral sloth and indifference can be overcome.

CHAPTER SEVEN

The Arenas of
Moral Action

A theory of moral experience approaches moral indifference by way of absences. By suggesting why moral experience succeeds, we hope to suggest why moral experience fails as well. A theory or idea about what makes ethics work is useful to the extent that it helps to illuminate situations of moral indifference. A useful theory helps us to ask the right questions and directs our attention to those absent elements that contribute to moral indifference. By identifying the absences that contribute to moral indifference, we obtain specific clues about what elements are required before moral commitment can be accomplished. Faced with a recalcitrant indifference, the theory proves its usefulness by suggesting specific ways and things we can do to alleviate moral sloth.

Moral issues may be grouped into three broad types or arenas: the political, the intermediate, and the personal. Although these three arenas are interconnected, they may nevertheless be distinguished for convenience. Applying the theory we have developed in the previous chapter, we will see that the nature of indifference and its possible remedy change according to the type or arena of issue being confronted. Moral commitment requires three key elements: experience, moral frameworks of interpretation, and power/embodiment. However, the element that is characteristically absent, and thus the form of indifference one typically confronts, varies from one arena to the next.

The Arenas of
Moral Indifference

The Political Arena. The political arena of moral action includes issues such as nuclear weapons, world hunger, economic and racial justice, environmental ethics, and policy issues at the national and international level. These issues characteristically invoke a notion that persons acting morally are participating citizens of a larger social or political entity beyond their own immediate face-to-face communities. Correspondingly, moral action in this arena is also less immediate or direct. An effective moral response to an environmental issue such as acid rain, for example, necessarily requires the enactment of legislation on a national or international level. The direct action of individuals in such instances is seldom effective. Moral imperatives in this arena call for indirect political responses to issues that are frequently long term and systemic in nature.

Faced with indifference to a moral issue in the political arena, we begin by looking for absences. What element is missing: experience, a morally informing framework of interpretation, or power/ embodiment? And second, what specific steps can be taken to supply that absent element in a way that will overcome moral sloth?

Typically, direct immediate experience with a political issue is rare. I may know intellectually that there is a threat of nuclear annihilation, but I do not experience that threat concretely. My drive to work each morning does not wind through a missile field or past radar installations. I do not know any military or scientific people who are in charge of the weapons, nor am I knowledgeable about the complex computer systems to which more and more control has been given. I have seen pictures of Hiroshima, but they seem very distant, with no more direct connection to me than pictures of the moon. I celebrate the establishment of a treaty eliminating a class of intermediate nuclear weapons, but I have not and will not experience the elimination of these arms in the same way that I will experience the removal of a tree stump in my front yard. In short, despite their global importance, I have no direct immediate experience of nuclear weapons. Mutually assured destruction exists, but the *is* I confront, my taken-for-granted reality, does not encompass nuclear war experientially. How or why should the issue of possible nuclear destruction concern me when I can neither hear, feel, taste, nor see its existence or threat? As with most issues of a political nature, I lack direct, immediate contact with the experience out of which the issue arises. As a consequence, the issue of possible nuclear destruction seems optional or inconsequential, even though it is neither.

In addition to a lack of experience, questions of interpretation (through what we have termed mythologies or ideologies of indifference) may enter into my indifference as well. If I am convinced that the threat of communist aggression is greater than the threat of deliberate or accidental nuclear war, then the possibility of that war is an acceptable risk. Similarly, our commitment to the myth of science is strong. Through science we created these weapons, so we tend to think that we can build enough safeguards through science to assure our own futures. Even if a nuclear exchange does occur, the exchange, many believe, can be limited. A limited exchange would surely destroy a city or two, but it would not, necessarily and inevitably, lead to the total destruction of a nuclear conflagration or a nuclear winter. The specter of nuclear destruction is literally unthinkable not only because we lack experience but also because of our commitment to the myth that "it can't happen." We think that no rational human being would ever "push the button." Moral indifference to the threat of nuclear arms is sustained if our commitment to the myth succeeds in persuading us that the *is* of nuclear weapons does not constitute an unmanageable moral problem.

In more immediate experience, a false or unworkable myth or ideology is undermined by experience itself. However, myths of indifference are especially persistent on the political level because there are seldom direct and determinant experiences to counteract them, especially in the short term. I never question the myth that the poor are lazy or mentally incompetent if I do not meet people who are poor. Experience is experience precisely when it calls into question our preconceived notions. The complex myth of technical mastery associated with nuclear weapons is seldom undermined directly in my experience and, if I ever experienced the failure of that myth, the results would be both catastrophic and irreversible. By the time I experience the failure of the nuclear myth, it will literally be "too late."

In addition to an absence of experience and the presence of anesthetizing frameworks of interpretation, moral impulses remain impotent apart from power/embodiment. On the political level, in particular, the issue of empowerment is a recurring source of moral indifference. Assume for the moment that the stockpiling of nuclear weapons is a problem and suppose, secondly, that I felt moved to do something about it. What would I do? What could I do to begin? Because political questions, by definition, involve large communities and their institutional and cultural expressions, the range of my power to affect change is always at issue; powerlessness is always a constant threat. It is one thing to change a specific item in the tax code, as difficult as that is, but it is something altogether different to change the military-industrial complex and the cultural suppositions that support it. Political support and legislative activity often take many years to accomplish; consequently, frustration at the pace or apparent lack of change is frequent. If I lack experience with nuclear weapons and other political issues, I also lack experience with how my actions can influence cultural norms and political policy. Lacking that experience, my indifference is sustained by the despairing notion epitomized by the question of the powerless, What can one person do?

Moral issues on the political level are especially vulnerable to the absences of experience and empowerment. To correct those absences, and the indifference that follows in their wake, requires that particular attention be paid to experience and to the techniques of empowerment. Thus, to continue our example, indifference to the issue of nuclear weapons can be diminished by exposing people to the statistics of nuclear weapons, including their numbers, costs, and potential for destruction. Additionally, by inviting people to experience imaginatively and vicariously the aftermath of nuclear war through films such as *The Day After* and *Testament* and by tracing the economic links between our normal day-to-day lives and the manufacture and distribution of nuclear weapons, we bring the issue closer to home. By making the abstract issue a concrete experience, we encourage people to confront the *is* of a nuclear-armed world. Such experience is crucial for, without it, the nuclear issue remains an avoidable condition, literally outside our experience. The nuclear issue begins with experience. Like many political issues, experience provides the impetus for moving beyond the inertia of indifference.

Confrontation with experience is the basis on which moral reflection must begin. To cite another example, suburbanites are stereotypically insulated from the experiences of poverty and homelessness. In Atlanta, this lack of experience is tested by a program in which persons from secure neighborhoods voluntarily become street people for several days to experience first hand the life of Atlanta's homeless. Similarly, a number of groups sponsor programs to third-world countries in order to bring the conditions of poverty and political oppression back home to America's tennis clubs and manicured lawns. One of the advantages of being middle class is that we have the ability, economically and socially, to avoid the experience of inadequate housing and sanitation, poor diets, and living on the margins of survival. The discrepancy between the *is* and the *ought* for the middle class is not great. Experientially confronting the *is* of the middle class with the *is* extant in the other America increases the perceived discrepancy between the *is* and the *ought* in a way that undermines moral sloth.

Indifference is nurtured by a sense of powerlessness as well as by a lack of experience. Powerlessness is lessened by showing and practicing the series of concrete, specific steps that can be taken to create and implement policy on a local or national level. Bread for the World is an exemplary citizen's lobby group in this regard—one that "thinks globally but acts locally." Bread for the World successfully reduces enormous problems such as world hunger to the doable step of writing a single letter to a representative or senator about a specific bill in Congress. Seventy-three million dollars was designated in our national budget for programs to alleviate hunger and malnutrition, in part because of the ninety thousand letters sent to Congress through such programs as "Offerings of Letters." By demonstrating how citizenship is a moral responsibility, Bread for the World tutors us in how a moral impetus to reduce hunger can be embodied and given power. One person cannot save the world but one person can write a letter, contribute to a lobby effort, compose a response to an editorial, talk openly to a neighbor about one's fears, or work with others for the election of a political candidate, and in other ways attempt to change public policy. By the practice of such single steps, the indifference of powerlessness and disembodied intentions is lessened.

The Personal Arena.   The second arena of moral practice is the personal level. This arena includes such questions as adultery, dishonesty, greed, lust, envy, and the like. Such questions reside at the opposite end of the spectrum from issues on the political level. At the political level, we often lack direct experience with an issue such as poverty or nuclear war. In contrast, our experience with envy or lust or personal dishonesty is perhaps too immediate. I do not need to read about the envy of a financially successful college roommate; I can experience it directly at my annual college reunion. Honesty in business is compromised by a deliberate posturing to establish a more favorable bargaining position with colleagues and clients alike. That is just part of doing business. Indifference to moral issues in instances such as these likely follows in the wake of too much, rather than too little, experience. Our immersion in unself-conscious day-to-day living, in conventional "everybody does it" morality, impedes the ability to see that other possibilities exist. We persistently experience a rising and falling sun even though we "know" better.

Immersed in our own limited experience, we are overwhelmed by the *is* in a way that subdues our awareness of a more problematic *ought.* Deprived and unconscious of that *ought,* we remain morally indifferent. If we characteristically lack experience of the *is* on the political level of moral activity, we most often lack the experience of the *ought,* of alternative ways of living and acting, on the personal level.

In the political arena, the indirectness of experience is mirrored by a similarly indirect means of embodiment or empowerment. In contrast, the direct realm of personal ethics involves a similarly immediate and direct correlation between our convictions and our actions. Adultery or fidelity, bigotry or tolerance, honesty or manipulation—each is constantly within my grasp. Indeed, I am enacting my convictions all the time, whether I do so deliberately or not. Specific situations may make it more or less likely that I will cheat a customer, but the power to do so or refrain from doing so is within me. I may not be very self-conscious and deliberate about my actions but, once awakened to their moral dimensions, I generally have the power to follow and to embody my deepest commitments.

In the personal arena then, we have ready access to experience and power/embodiment. The persistence of indifference in this arena, therefore, suggests that its source may lie primarily in the mythic, in the ways we interpret our experience morally. Persons are indifferent on the personal realm of moral activity because either they hold onto myths of indifference or because, in their aversion to moralism and to a general uncertainty about right and wrong, they have lost their morally sustaining myths altogether.

If, for example, I believe in the myth of personal freedom, in a doctrine of individual growth, expression, and exploration, then I will be less likely to suffer the restrictions imposed by marital fidelity. Within such a framework, morals will seldom extend beyond the negative boundary of "doing no harm." Similarly, if I can be persuaded that it is a dog-eat-dog world, that the world is essentially competitive and amoral, then I am not dissuaded from taking a competitive advancement whenever or wherever one might present itself. What do greed and envy mean in the context of the American story of success? Ethics in a competitive, amoral context becomes a "liability," something that actually lessens my chances for success, rather than a means to a better life.

When we are lured by the myths of indifference, our better impulses are starved by the lack of sustaining myths of commitment. Indeed, most people are greatly uncertain about what constitutes "goodness," so much so that they have altogether gotten out of the habit of thinking morally. Indeed, in most instances, thinking morally has become slightly embarrassing. Moral arguments are the last arguments raised and the first to be dismissed. The connections between public and private morality are weak in a way that permits us to dismiss the latter as unimportant. Inconvenienced by a moral imperative, we hear ourselves saying that greed is either a matter of opinion or private vice, without public importance. Worse yet, we catch ourselves condemning greed on the one hand and fantasizing about the life-styles of the rich and famous on the other. Without sustaining myths of commitment, morality is finally as meaningless as the nihilists have claimed. If morality makes no difference, if it is not grounded in some ultimate truth, then little stands between my action and expediency or impulse.

Whether one defines the problem in terms of myths of indifference or an absence of myths of commitment, the solution to inadequate frameworks of interpretation is not entirely clear. The deliberate, self-conscious invention of such culturally sustaining myths is as problematic as it is needed. We are, as someone has said, between the death of the old gods and the birth of the new. There is certainly widespread recognition that problems exist and that the old myths of individualism and value-neutrality are failing us on both corporate and individual levels. People express a longing for what Morris Berman describes as "the reenchantment of the world" but a consensus about how we are to get from here to there has yet to be achieved. The reinstatement of a value-laden universe as persistently argued by Houston Smith in *Beyond the Post-Modern Mind* and as echoed in Robert Bellah's, et al., *Habits of the Heart* and William M. Sullivan's *Reconstructing Public Philosophy* are enormously attractive, but connecting those visions to contemporary American life and institutions remains a long-term problem. Fundamentalists have chosen to turn back the clock as a means of avoiding the undermining effects of pluralism and modernity. In so doing, however, they have compartmentalized life and established merely a temporary holding position against what seems to be the tide of history. Two things are equally clear. On the one hand, without some degree of cultural consensus, myths are tentative and fleeting and essentially avoidable while, on the other hand, the task of creating such a consensus remains a central task in undermining the basis of moral indifference.

The Intermediate Arena.   The third level of moral practice occurs on the intermediate level. The intermediate level includes such issues as business or professional ethics, the ethics of churches, academic communities, and corporations, as well as racial and gender subcommunities. Moral issues in this arena are intermediate precisely because they are in between the direct experience and control of ethics in the personal arena and the far more abstract and indirect moral practice found in the political arena. Ethics in this arena involves commerce with a subcommunity or volunteer association, with a group that is larger than one's immediate family but smaller than the *civitas* institutionalized in politics. Moral loyalties in this arena are, almost by definition, divided between self, subcommunity, and the larger commonweal. Membership and participation in the subcommunities of the intermediate arena are typically voluntary without being guaranteed. My moral participation in the individual and civic arenas is inescapable in a way that my participation in the moral community of business or church is voluntary and freely chosen.

Imagine for a moment the recurring questions that occur in business ethics. Is what a business pays its employees a moral issue? If a corporation exports its manufacturing plants to a third-world country, if a toy manufacturer closely links its products to Saturday morning television programs—are these specifically moral issues? When or how are business decisions made on the basis of morality? What is the relationship between the good of business and the good of the commonweal? Moralists who confront businesses with such questions are frequently met with either puzzlement or outright indifference. What does the theory we have outlined suggest about the source of, and remedy for, such recalcitrant indifference? Businessmen and businesswomen are our neighbors, friends, and family members. Most of them are good, moral people on both the individual and civic levels. When confronted on the morality of their business practices, however, they may exhibit a strange and venomous form of indifference that requires explanation.

Experience, moral frameworks of interpretation, and power/ embodiment make their contributions to indifference in the intermediate arena of moral practice. Not surprisingly, the nature of those contributions is similar to those in the personal and political arenas, depending on which end of the spectrum the specific issue in question is nearest. In some instances, for example, the actions of a manager or CEO may approach the direct experience and power of implementation characteristic of ethics in the personal realm. In other instances, however, an engineer may have little direct authority or power to implement his concerns about the safety of a product. To change things, he or she may have to become engaged in intramural politics. As we will now see, the search for absences, the persistent question, What absent element leads to moral indifference? begins with distinguishing those occasions when one is or is not a participant in the community in which a moral issue has arisen.

The Indifference of the Nonparticipant

Moral situations about which it can be said that I am not a participant most clearly come to light in areas of technical and scientific expertise. Should the space shuttle *Challenger* have been launched in light of the potential problems with the O-rings? Are the risks of using nuclear energy or a new pesticide acceptable in relation to the potential benefits? Should bypass surgery be used on an elderly heart patient despite the risks? Is the domestic policy of Nicaragua morally acceptable? These are practical questions with moral dimensions about which, as one who is outside the political, scientific, and medical communities in which they arise, I can seemingly contribute little. The vast majority of such questions arise and subside on a routine basis, necessarily, outside my attention or knowledge. Indifference to the moral dilemma of communities in which I am not a participant is based on a profound lack of experience. Without such experience, I am unable to determine what a potentially moral situation is, much less what it ought to be.

Besides an absence of experience, indifference to situations in which I am not a participant is secondarily sustained by an absence of power to embody or to enact directly my vision of what ought to be. I have little, if any, influence on the moral choices of an engineer working in the corridors of NASA or the Ford Motor Company, or on the medical decisions of a physician at Crawford Long Hospital or a government official in Managua. Decisions with moral dimensions are made daily, but they are beyond my awareness or influence. Occasionally, the moral questions of an engineer, physician, or bureaucrat may be raised to a more general or political level of public policy or regulation. In such cases, I may be able to exert influence indirectly in the political arena. On the intermediate level of moral action, however, my ability to enact moral choices on communities in which I do not participate is, almost by definition, severely limited. If I am not omniscient, neither am I omnipotent.

Importantly, if I am unable to affect the moral decisions of the engineer, physician, or bureaucrat, I am also seldom directly and immediately affected by those decisions. If an engineer compromises a design in order to stay within budget, if an elderly patient is allowed to die, if a government program suppresses the development of indigenous agriculture, I generally do not have to pay the consequences. Moral outrage is an easy and self-satisfying virtue when, as a nonparticipant, I do not have to pay the price of a moral decision. Moral condemnation of the military-industrial complex becomes more difficult if, with the cancellation of a defense contract, one's father or brother or spouse will be laid off, if one will suffer directly the consequences and dislocations of unemployment. The legitimacy of my deliberations on moral issues lessens in proportion to the distance between me and the consequences of choosing one moral position rather than another.

If the moral situations of communities in which I do not participate are largely outside my experience and power, and if the consequences of a moral decision within those communities do not affect me, then are such situations my concern? Given the limitations inherent with my status as an outsider, should I be concerned with the decisions of the scientist, physician, or bureaucrat? Moral commitment or indifference is often based on how one defines the boundary between the participant and the nonparticipant, put another way, on the old question: Am I my brother's keeper? This is a question of myth and interpretation in which the boundaries between participant and nonparticipant are constantly changing. Until *Silent Spring,* the use of pesticides was a question for scientists and farmers. Until *Unsafe at Any Speed,* car design was confined to the engineers at Ford and GM. Until the civil rights movement, the treatment of blacks was a problem limited to the black community. Moral commitment often begins at the point that someone else's problem becomes my problem in a way that obscures the demarcation between participant and nonparticipant. Myths upholding the autonomy of subcommunities sustain indifference, whereas myths that link the actions of all to the general commonweal encourage commitment.

Overcoming indifference to the moral situation of communities in which I do not participate requires experience, albeit as a participant-observer, and a clearer sense of how the actions of the scientist, say, are connected with my own vision of the commonweal. In this case as in others, supplying the absence of experience, power, and inadequate myths is a recurring theme, based as it is on a presumption against indifference. In situations in which we are not participants, however, that presumption may be questioned or at least advanced with caution. Put another way, indifference may actually be desirable in situations where it leaves me time for other moral commitments, especially when it focuses my attention on those concerns indigenous to my own moral community.

As human beings, our time is limited. No one can confront every moral problem; no one can be universally concerned about every moral dilemma. We necessarily must pick and choose our battles. Given the inherent absence of experience and power I possess whenever I am an outsider, my indifference to the moral situation of the physician or the Nicaraguan bureaucrat may provide a clue to an instance when I am appropriately disqualified from becoming morally involved. By remaining indifferent to the moral situation of the engineer, I am given time to examine the moral issues that arise in situations where I have both more direct experience and the ability to empower/embody my moral vision. Indeed, involvement in the moral situations of physicians and nuclear scientists may often be a means of avoiding moral issues closer to home. My moral outrage at the immorality of a scientist working on Star Wars may feel good in proportion to the degree that it is literally inconsequential to my day-in, day-out experience. Attention to Star Wars is used as an apologetic for my indifference to issues that are closer at hand. Moral commitment is hard enough in the best of circumstances; commitment to issues that arise within communities in which I am not a direct participant are doubly impeded by an absence of experience and power/embodiment.

The Indifference of the Participant

In contrast to nonparticipants, participants within a moral community are most often indifferent because they do not interpret their activities as "moral." Indifference is not due to the absence of experience or power but to a persistent tendency to see the institutions in which we participate as somehow morally neutral. In business, for example, the myth of neutrality persuades us that the activity of business is largely outside the realm of the moralists. Largely successfully, the myth of neutrality separates our participation in business or the professions from our participation in personal or civic arenas of morality. As a result, we fail to acknowledge that a business is a moral as well as a commercial entity.

Businesses, no less than churches or universities, are structured for the achievement of certain ends. In pursuit of those ends, the institutionalized corporate culture encourages or inhibits specific behaviors. Stereotypically, the business community rewards ambition, rationality, and discipline rather than empathy, compassion, and spontaneity. Businesses help create certain kinds of people in a way that is no less moral than the formation of character evinced by the church or university. Corporate culture contains a whole universe of formal and customary *oughts,* but these *oughts* are most often hidden from our attention by a pervasive myth of neutrality. We are indifferent because the institutional locus of our activities is conceived to be neutral and thus outside conventional moral imperatives.

Closely related to the myth of neutrality is the myth of professionalization. The myth of professionalization encourages us to identify our activity with the values of the subgroup rather than with personal values or the imperatives of the entire civic community. The chemists working on gas warfare may safely insulate themselves from the final morality of research by focusing on the isolated technical questions of chemical reactions. Albert Speer's identification as a technician and architect permitted him to ignore his intimate involvement in the Nazi Holocaust. By convincing us that our primary loyalty is to a business, university, or other subcommunity, the myth of professionalization, like the myth of neutrality, supports our indifference to the potential claims of personal or civic virtue. Overcoming indifference, in turn, begins with a debunking of the myths of neutrality and professionalization and a corresponding reemergence of a mythic interpretative framework that can successfully integrate the moral activities of the subgroup with the personal and civic arenas of moral virtue.

Of course, there are many people whose commitment to personal or civic virtue is greater than their commitment to the ethos of the subgroup. "Whistle-blowers," people who divulge—often at great personal risk—the unethical or illegal practices of an institution are exemplary in this regard. By attracting the attention of the community at large, the whistle-blower transmutes an intramural action into a public political issue. The person of moral conscience within an institution has a peculiarly difficult problem of power and embodiment. How does the moral critic of a community act on his or her convictions without being excluded from the very community he or she wishes to change? Prophets have no honor in their own country. Thus persons of good will remain indifferent, at least functionally, because how they can go about changing the institutions in which they participate is unclear. Often, changing other institutions is less threatening than changing the institutions in which one is most directly involved. Because participation in a business community is a privilege, in the sense that one can be fired if the moral imperatives of the business are not followed, the employee's ability to act on the basis of personal or civic virtue is compromised. In addition to overcoming the myths of neutrality and professionalization then, overcoming indifference on the intermediate level requires especially subtle forms of embodiment and power, the nature of which changes according to the specific issue and community in which one participates.

The Arenas of Commitment

Dividing ethics into civic, personal, and intermediate arenas is arbitrary, of course. The hunger issue, for example, engages all three arenas. In the personal arena, this issue asks how we spend our money and on what products. In the intermediate arena, it asks how the church uses its resources, both educational and financial, to alleviate hunger. In the civic arena, it questions the effects of budget and tax policy on the needy. In each arena, the outline of our theory suggests that, by being attentive to absences, we can identify that element or combination of elements—whether experience, interpretation, or power/embodiment—that most contributes to moral indifference. In one instance, overcoming indifference requires working in a soup kitchen to gain experience with the *is* of poverty. In another instance, it requires freeing oneself from the mythic notion that hunger is an accident of nature. In yet a third instance, overcoming indifference requires learning more about a specific piece of legislation dealing with school lunch programs. Theories do not in themselves solve problems, but theories can point us in the right direction. In this case, a theory of moral indifference helps us to see the black holes whose absences define the sources of moral indifference, whether they occur in the personal, political, or intermediate realms of moral action. Exchanging the absence for the presence of experience, acquiring morally committing frameworks of interpretation, and acting in light of power/embodiment—these steps create a basis for seeing, acknowledging, and acting in response to moral imperatives.

CHAPTER EIGHT

Ethics and the Rhetoric
of Indifference

Ethics is reflection on inaction, a discipline attentive to absences. We swim in an ocean of moral currents but, like fish in the sea, we do so unwittingly. Our day-in, day-out, taken-for-granted experience seldom seems or feels like a moral struggle, much less a decisive conflict between good and evil. Choosing which brand of catsup to buy at the supermarket, watering the front yard, playing tennis on the weekend—conventionally at least, these are not the topics about which moralists debate. Moral issues are as close at hand as the Tuesday evening PTA meeting but, more often than not, their moral currents are unheeded. Instead, the moral situations most typical of the middle class are exchanged for the adventurous pursuit of more interesting moral debates about South Africa, liberation theology, or genetic engineering. Like all adventurers, however, ethical adventurers are absent from home, and their short-lived explorations seldom affect their daily round of activities. The moral life is a way of keeping score, a means for infusing actions with meaning, direction, and a sense of drama. The absence of moral life is, as Robert Frost said of poetry, "like playing tennis without a net."

In his classic essay, "The Will to Believe," William James provides an analysis of belief that is also applicable to moral commitment. As such, it provides a closing perspective on the previous reflections on moral indifference. A genuine decision, James writes, presents a choice between options that are at one and the same time alive, forced, and momentous.

Options are alive or dead according to our willingness to act on them. Hypotheses beyond the realm of the possible or credible are

117

like disconnected electrical connections—dead and lifeless. The option to become a Mahdi fails to scintillate because, James observes, it lies beyond our experience, whereas the option to become an agnostic makes at least some appeal to our imaginations. Agnosticism, because of our experiences and frameworks of interpretation, is at least a comprehensible option, whereas becoming a Mahdi makes no sense, no electrical connection, at all.

To be genuine, options must be not only alive but forced. Forced options are those that are unavoidable; with forced options, James says, "there is no standing place outside of one or the other alternative." Faced with whether or not to take an umbrella outside with me, I can avoid the decision altogether by staying home. In contrast, the decision to accept either the truth or to go without it leaves no other alternative. Not to decide in such instances is nevertheless a decision to maintain the status quo. One either decides to kill oneself or one decides to live, according to Camus. There is no middle or neutral ground to the most fundamental question of philosophy.

Genuine decisions must be momentous as well as alive and forced. Momentous options represent unique opportunities. Momentous decisions are contrasted by James with those more trivial decisions in which an opportunity is not unique, when the stakes are insignificant, or when the decision is reversible. An invitation to join a polar expedition is momentous, according to James, because one is not likely to receive another such invitation. Scientific hypotheses, on the other hand, are trivial because they can be abandoned if proven inadequate.

Concerning the phenomenon of moral indifference, James's categories suggest that ethicists face a rhetorical problem. Persons are indifferent, in part, because moral questions are asked or presented in the wrong way. Persons are indifferent because they are not persuaded that the questions addressed to them by ethicists are genuine in the sense that James employed the term. The failure of ethics in America is a failure of moral practice, but it is also a failure in the rhetorical strategy of ethicists. Overcoming indifference requires a rhetorical strategy for convincing people that moral options are indeed "genuine"—that is, alive, forced, and momentous.

Consider for the moment the currently popular phrase "option for the poor." At first glance, how genuine is that option for the middle class? First, is it really an alive option? Is the voluntary abandonment of the middle class's privileged position a real possibility on which people are willing to act? How many people can actually or realistically consider sacrificing the education or nutrition of their own children in order to support the children of the homeless? Second, is the option forced? I may or may not help the poor, but I may also remain indifferent or decide that my energies are better spent working for a nuclear-free environment. The pluralism available to the middle class is a context for avoiding forced options, moral or otherwise. And third, how momentous is the option for the poor from the perspective of the middle class? My decision may be significant but it is certainly not, from my perspective, irreversible or unique. I may work for the poor today, but I may just as easily not work for them tomorrow. I can postpone my commitment indefinitely, seemingly with impunity, because the option is always available to me.

Overcoming indifference toward the option for the poor requires persuading people that the question is a genuine option. Voluntarily accepting a lower standard of living for myself and my children may be beyond the realm of what I would be willing to do, but I may nevertheless be challenged by other options on which I would be willing to act. I may not be willing to reduce my standard of living, but I may be convinced to work one night a week in a family shelter. The option for the poor may not seem forced, at least not initially. But if I can be persuaded that my fate and the fate of the poor are connected, then I will finally have to realize that if I am not part of the solution then I am part of the problem. Moral commitment requires acknowledging that one is either moving ahead or moving backwards; there is no resting place, no middle or neutral ground. And finally, accepting the option for the poor may not seem irreversible and momentous from my perspective, but from the perspective of those thousands of children who die every day from malnutrition, my continued inaction for even one additional day is irreversible and unique. My response is embodied, if not obviously in my life then in the lives of those whom I do not help. Moral reflection succeeds in challenging our indifference only when we are convinced that the questions or options it raises are genuine.

The reflections of James on the nature of belief help make explicit an underlying argument of the foregoing work. The failure of ethics in America is a failure of practice, but it is also a failure in the rhetorical strategy of ethicists. Persons are indifferent because the ethics written by academic ethicists is not, in the main, rhetorically compelling. Ethics will become more compelling to the extent that it becomes more adept at identifying and supplying the absences present in indifference. Ethics must begin with reflection on, and a rhetorical response to, the phenomenon of moral indifference. Why are people uninterested? In contrast to those who would presume an interested audience, the ethicist of absences begins with a moral apologetic.

Moral indifference, as seen in chapter 2, is a deep-seated tendency toward sloth. Variously described as a case of arrested development, existential anxiety, or defective love, indifference is a persistent and universal inclination toward sloth. Nevertheless, indifference is neither natural nor inevitable. We do not possess a gene for indifference in the same way that we possess genes for blue eyes and five fingers. We acquire, we learn indifference; indifference is a human artifact. Because indifference is artificial, its presence is attributable to discernible causes. Why are people morally indifferent? I suggested in the introduction that indifference can be attributed to an absence of seeing, acknowledging, or power/embodiment.

In the first instance, failure to see can be overcome by responding to an absence of experience. Experience may be lacking for either the *is* or the *ought* of moral insight. In chapter 7, I argued that such experience can be either direct or imaginative. People fail to respond to the poor because they have no experience with the *is* of poverty. Living comfortably in the suburbs, the middle class is safely insulated from experiencing the starchy diets and crowded, often dangerous, living conditions of the poor.

Alternatively, people remain indifferent because they lack experience with the *ought* conveyed by a moral vision. People are impoverished, but a moral vision persuades us that such poverty is neither necessary nor desirable. Things can and should be different. Moral *oughts* provide the foundation on which an experiential discrepancy between the *is* and the *ought* of moral insight is based.

People may have direct or imaginative experience of the poor and yet continue to be indifferent. In addition to experience, commitment requires moral frameworks of interpretation. Such frameworks help us to see and to acknowledge our responsibility toward the poor. On the negative side, in chapters 3, 4, and 5, respectively, I analyzed illustrative mythologies of indifference current in popular religion, culture, and political ideology. In instances where we are bewitched by these mythologies of indifference, moral commitment requires a deliberate, self-conscious process of debunking our comforting beliefs. More positively, however, the presence of mythologies of indifference suggests the absence of, and thus need for, compelling mythologies of commitment as articulated in such recent works as *Habits of the Heart* and *Reconstructing Public Philosophy*. Ethics will become more compelling to the extent that it addresses the mythological dimensions of moral indifference and commitment and how, in turn, such myths contribute to an acknowledgment of our moral responsibility toward others.

Finally, moral commitments must be embodied/powered. Moral insight and ownership are merely self-gratifying forms of sentimentalism or bazaar forms of entertainment apart from power/embodiment. The *telos* or goal of seeing and acknowledging is moral action. The connection between moral commitments and power/embodiment works both ways. On the one hand, people must be persuaded that all social arrangements are, inescapably, embodiments of power and moral commitments. On the other hand, people must also be persuaded and instructed about how they can embody their best impulses in concrete actions for the good.

The telling absence—whether of experience, committing frameworks of interpretation, or power/embodiment—typically changes as one moves from one realm of moral activity to the next. In chapter 8, I briefly applied the theory developed in chapter 7 to the individual, political, and intermediate arenas of moral activity. We saw, for example, how the absence of experience is a constant threat to moral indifference in the political arena, whereas the absence of morally informing frameworks of interpretation often contributes to moral indifference in the individual arena. Our application of the theory is in no sense complete; nevertheless, it is illustrative of how indifference may be initially approached and challenged in three typical arenas of moral action.

Rhetorically, ethicists will succeed to the extent that they provide or compensate for the absences contributing to indifference. The best ethicists and ethical journals have always done this. Ethics has overcome indifference whenever it has integrated experiential descriptions, compelling interpretations, and concrete guidelines for action. By supplying a theoretical account rooted in absences, the rhetorical strategy implicit in the best ethical practice becomes more visible.

Indifference is the most persistent problem in ethics. It is the beginning point from which moral reflection must begin. Most people could not care less about moral deliberations. Indifference, hardness of heart, apathy, moral sloth, caring less, are problematic because we live in an imperfect world. In a perfect world, indifference would not be a problem. In our world, however, indifference is never morally innocent. Until the eschaton, indifference remains a central, if often overlooked, aspect of the moral life. The liturgical confession "we have not loved our neighbors as ourselves" becomes a moral question: What are the things we have left undone; what are we missing? Ethics is a search for absences, a reflection on inaction.

BIBLIOGRAPHY

CHAPTER TWO

Baum, Gregory. *Religion and Alienation*. New York: Paulist Press, 1975.

Campbell, Joseph. *Myths to Live By*. New York: Bantam Books, 1972.

Dunfee, Susan Nelson. "The Sin of Hiding: A Feminist Critique of Reinhold Niebuhr's Account of the Sin of Pride." *Soundings* 65 (Fall 1982): 316–27.

Fairlie, Henry. *The Seven Deadly Sins Today*. Notre Dame, Ind.: University of Notre Dame Press, 1979.

Grant, Brian W. *From Sin to Wholeness*. Philadelphia: Westminster Press, 1982.

Green, Marjorie. *The Knower and the Known*. New York: Basic Books, 1966. The quotation is found on page 160.

Lyman, Stanford M. *The Seven Deadly Sins*. New York: St. Martin's Press, 1978.

May, William F. *A Catalogue of Sins*. New York: Holt, Rinehart, and Winston, 1967.

Niebuhr, Reinhold. *The Nature and Destiny of Man*. Vols. 1 and 2. New York: Charles Scribner's Sons, 1941–43, 1963.

————. *The Self and the Dramas of History*. New York: Charles Scribner's Sons, 1955.

Raines, John C. "Sin as Pride and Sin as Sloth." *Christianity and Crisis* 29 (February 3, 1969) 4–8.

Schell, Jonathan. *The Fate of the Earth*. New York: Avon Books, 1982. The quotation is found on page 151.

CHAPTER THREE

Coleman, Richard J. *Issues of Theological Conflict*. Grand Rapids: Wm. B. Eerdmans, 1980.

Henry, Paul B. *Politics for Evangelicals.* Valley Forge, Pa.: Judson Press, 1974.

Miller, Donald E. "The Future of Liberal Christianity." *The Christian Century* 99 (March 10, 1982) 266–70.

Moberg, David O. *The Great Reversal: Evangelism versus Social Concern.* New York and Philadelphia: J. B. Lippincott, 1972.

Ochs, Peter. "The Religion of Liberal Humanity." *The NICM Journal* 8 (Spring & Summer, 1983) 93–105.

Pierard, Richard V. *The Unequal Yoke: Evangelical Christianity and Political Conservatism.* New York and Philadelphia: J. B. Lippincott, 1970.

Rauschenbusch, Walter. *A Theology for the Social Gospel.* New York: Macmillan Co., 1918.

Smith, Timothy L. *Revivalism and Social Reform: American Protestantism on the Eve of the Civil War.* Gloucester, Mass.: Peter Smith, 1976.

Woodbridge, John D., Mark A. Noll, and Nathan O. Hatch. *The Gospel in America.* Grand Rapids: Zondervan, 1979.

Wallis, Jim. *The Call to Conversion.* San Francisco: Harper & Row, 1982.

CHAPTER FOUR

Berger, Peter L. *A Rumor of Angels: Modern Society and the Rediscovery of the Supernatural.* Garden City, N.Y.: Doubleday Co., 1969.

Browne, Ray B., Marshall Fishwick, and Michael T. Marsden. *Heroes of Popular Culture.* Bowling Green, Ohio: Bowling Green University Popular Press, 1972.

Estes, Ted L. "The Inenarrable Contraption: Reflections on the Metaphor of Story." *Journal of the American Academy of Religion* 52 (September 1974), 415–34. The quotation is found on page 420.

Fishwick, Marshall W. *Common Culture and the Great Tradition.* Westport, Conn.: Greenwood Press, 1982.

Huber, Richard M. *The American Idea of Success.* Buffalo: McGraw-Hill Books, 1971.

Jewett, Robert, and John Shelton Lawrence. *The American Monomyth.* Garden City, N.Y.: Doubleday Books, Anchor, 1977. The quotation is found on page 59.

Nelson, John Wiley. *Your God Is Alive and Well and Appearing in Popular Culture.* Philadelphia: Westminster Press, 1976.

Novak, Michael. *The Experience of Nothingness.* New York: Harper & Row, 1971.

————. *Ascent of the Mountain, Flight of the Dove.* New York: Harper & Row, 1971. The quotation is found on page 63.

Scott, Nathan A. Jr., "The Rediscovery of Story in Recent Theology and the Refusal of Story in Recent Literature." *JAAR Thematic Studies* 49 (1983): 139–55. The quotation is found on page 142.

Wright, Will. *Six Guns and Society: A Structural Study of the Western.* Berkeley: University of California Press, 1975.

CHAPTER FIVE

Adler, Mortimer J. *Six Great Ideas*. New York: Macmillan, 1981.
_____. *Ten Philosophical Mistakes*. New York: Macmillan, 1985.
Baumer, Franklin Le Van. *Religion and the Rise of Skepticism*. New York: Harcourt, Brace & World, 1960.
Berger, Peter L. *Pyramids of Sacrifice: Political Ethics and Social Change*. New York: Basic Books, 1984.
Callahan, Daniel. *The Tyranny of Survival*. New York: Macmillan, 1973.
Campbell, Joseph. *Myths to Live By*. New York: Viking Press, 1972.
Caplan, Arthur L., and Daniel Callahan, eds. *Ethics in Hard Times*. New York: Plenum Press, 1981.
Friedman, Maurice. *To Deny Our Nothingness*. New York: Dell Publishing, 1967.
Fromm, Erich. *Escape from Freedom*. New York: Holt, Rinehart, and Winston, 1941.
Gilkey, Langdon. *Naming the Whirlwind: The Renewal of God-Language*. New York and Indianapolis: Bobbs-Merrill, 1969.
MacIntyre, Alasdair. *After Virtue*. Notre Dame, Ind.: University of Notre Dame Press, 1981.
Rieff, Philip. *The Triumph of the Therapeutic*. New York: Macmillan, 1973.
Sandel, Michael J. *Liberalism and the Limits of Justice*. Cambridge: Cambridge University Press, 1982.
Sullivan, William M. *Reconstructing Public Philosophy*. Berkeley: University of California Press, 1982.
Will, George F. *Statecraft as Soulcraft*. New York: Simon & Schuster, 1983.
Wogaman, J. Philip. *The Great Economic Debate*. Philadelphia: Westminster Press, 1977.

CHAPTER SIX

Alves, Rubem A. "Some Thoughts on a Program for Ethics." *Union Seminary Quarterly Review* 26 (Winter 1971): 153–70. The quotation is found on page 159.
Bellah, Robert N., Richard Madsen, William M. Sullivan, Ann Swidler, and Steven M. Tipton. *Habits of the Heart*. Berkeley: University of California Press, 1985.
Berman, Morris. *The Reenchantment of the World*. Ithaca, N.Y.: Cornell University Press, 1981.
Birch, Bruce C., and Larry L. Rasmussen. *The Predicament of the Prosperous*. Philadelphia: Westminster Press, 1978.
Burrell, David, and Stanley Hauerwas. "Self-Deception and Autobiography: Theological and Ethical Reflections on Speer's *Inside the Third Reich*." *Journal of Religious Ethics* 2 (1974): 99–117.
Dewey, John. *Art as Experience*. New York: G. P. Putnam's Sons, 1934, (1958).

Green, Marjorie. *The Knower and the Known*. New York: Basic Books, 1966. The quotation is found on page 160.

Hauerwas, Stanley. *Vision and Virtue*. Notre Dame, Ind.: Fides Publishing Inc., 1974.

Hoehn, Richard A. *Up from Apathy*. Nashville: Abingdon Press, 1983. The quotations are found on pages 87 and 99.

James, William. *The Will to Believe and Other Essays in Popular Philosophy*. New York: Dover Publications, 1956.

Smith, Houston. *Beyond the Post-Modern Mind*. New York: Crossroad, 1982.

Sullivan, William M. *Reconstructing Public Philosophy*. Berkeley: University of California Press, 1982.

CHAPTER EIGHT

James, William. "The Will to Believe," *The Will to Believe and Other Essays in Popular Philosophy*. New York: Dover Publications, 1956.

INDEX